BRIC+S

A short exploration of the BRICS alliance

Adithya Vikram Sakthivel

CONTENTS

INTRODUCTION

The BRICS, an acronym that resonates with a potent sense of optimism and national pride, especially among fervent nationalists within the political and economic elite of some of its member states. It stands as an emblem of unity, a symbol of hope, and a rallying point for those who perceive it as a potentially formidable force in the evolving global multi-polar landscape. But what precisely is this multinational group? To truly grasp the essence of this so-called economic alliance, we must delve into its origins, objectives, and the intricate dynamics that underpin its existence.

The first step in unravelling the BRICS phenomenon is to clearly define the member nations of this grouping of countries. As stated earlier, the BRICS is an acronym formed from the names of its member states, namely the Federative Republic of Brazil (Brazil), The Russian Federation (Russia), the Republic of India (India), the People's Republic of China (China), and the Republic of South Africa (South Africa). These five nations, each distinctive in its own right, collectively constitute the backbone of this economic alliance. It's noteworthy that the BRICS alliance spans almost every major economic region in the world. Brazil represents the vibrant economies of the Americas, while Russia used to hold a prominent place in Europe and Eurasia. India and China, two economic powerhouses, serve as the stalwarts of the Asia-Pacific region. Completing this diverse ensemble, South Africa stands as the representative from the continent of Africa. This geographical diversity not only underscores the global reach of BRICS but also highlights the strategic importance of these nations in shaping the future of the world economy.

If one was to ask a random person on the bustling streets of New Delhi or amid the vibrant energy of Rio De Janeiro, their response might typically lean towards a nonchalant "don't know, don't care," or a more aggressive response of "do I look like I give a damn." However, when engaging with more politically informed individuals, particularly those with strong nationalistic leanings, you're likely to encounter a perception that BRICS resembles a figurative messiah, one destined to deliver the developing world from the perceived horrors of an economic world order led by the United States, wielding control through the dominance of the dollar as the reserve currency. A slightly more liberal-minded person might suggest that BRICS serves as an alternative economic counterweight to Western economic institutions, capable of coexisting and operating independently of these more established organisations.

Yet, upon conducting a more comprehensive analysis of the diverse perspectives held by various individuals toward this group of nations, it becomes an enigma—a reflection of what each questioned individual subconsciously wishes to be true. In this sense, BRICS is as much a canvas for projecting aspirations as it is a concrete alliance. However, this brings us back to the fundamental question: What truly defines BRICS? This book endeavours to embark on an intellectual journey, one that explores the origins and activities of this multifaceted organisation, aiming not only to decode its objectives but also to discern its evolving role in a rapidly changing global landscape. As we navigate this exploration, we will uncover the historical underpinnings, the geopolitical intricacies, and the economic ambitions that have brought these nations together. By the end, we hope to offer a definitive understanding of BRICS, unravelled from the myriad perspectives and uncertainties that shroud its existence.

PREFACE

In the ever-evolving geopolitical landscape of the present day, it is imperative to acknowledge that the world order is in a perpetual state of transformation. What is considered the norm today may cease to be the status quo in the future.

With this understanding, this book endeavours to provide the most accurate insights possible. However, it is essential to recognize that the predictions and events discussed within may undergo changes. As of the time of writing, which is in early October 2023, the information contained herein is as precise as the author can reasonably ensure.

CHAPTER 1

The Father

The BRICS, despite often being hailed by many fervent nationalists and anti-Western elements within several member nations as an ensemble akin to Marvel Comics' Avengers, rallying together to combat the perceived evils of dollar reserve currencies, Western-led economic growth, free trade capitalism, and globalisation, had a rather unassuming origin. The inception of BRICS can be traced back to a report published by the then-chairman of Goldman Sachs Asset Management, Jim O'Neill.

The irony of this somewhat anticlimactic origin story is something that even the most ardent BRICS enthusiasts tend to overlook, as it deviates from the simplistic narrative of good versus evil, or strong versus weak, that they often project upon the BRICS grouping. However, from an academic and economic perspective, it's widely acknowledged that Jim O'Neill is the first recorded individual to propose the concept of a grouping of emerging economies, which eventually paved the way for the creation of the BRICS.

This origin story challenges the conventional expectations of grandeur and heroism often associated with geopolitical alliances, instead highlighting the role of economic pragmatism and foresight in shaping the course of global economic affairs. It underscores the complexity and nuance inherent in international relations, where even seemingly heroic narratives can have their roots in the world of finance, projected growth, and macroeconomic factors.

The initial report that set in motion a series of events leading to the eventual establishment of the BRICS organisation was published in 2001 by Terence James O'Neill, more commonly known as Jim O'Neil, who also currently holds the honorary position of professor of economics at the University of Manchester. In this groundbreaking report, O'Neil identified four countries that, at that time, stood at a similar stage of newly advanced economic development. These "big 4" were Brazil, Russia, India, and China, forming the memorable acronym BRIC.

O'Neil's initial thesis report, based on data from 2001, predicted that these four nations would emerge as some of the most influential players in global trade by the year 2050. The rationale behind this prediction was compelling at the time of its initial publication, as these countries collectively represented over a quarter of the world's landmass and were home to close to 40% of the global population. Jim O'Neil's foresight in recognizing the potential of these emerging economies marked a pivotal moment in the evolution of global economic thought.

While Jim O'Neil's visionary thinking and economic predictions were revolutionary, it's important to note that his thesis on the BRIC grouping of nations primarily relied on purely theoretical economic indicators. His report, at its core, aimed to provide insight into promising emerging markets and was primarily conceived as an analysis report to guide potential investors seeking opportunities in these burgeoning economies.

O'Neil's groundbreaking work didn't inherently propose or imply that the "big 4" should immediately form an economic alliance of their own. Instead, it was a forward-looking analysis that illuminated the potential growth and significance of Brazil, Russia, India, and China as individual economic entities. His emphasis was on their promising prospects as separate markets, each offering distinct opportunities for investment and growth at the time of publishing.

It's worth noting that Jim O'Neil, despite his reputation for revolutionary economic thinking, had a tendency to group emerging economies into catchy-sounding acronyms without always taking into account the complexities of geographical, social, cultural, and political factors. One of his later works, dating back to around 2013, introduced the concept of the MINT countries, which comprised Mexico, Indonesia, Nigeria, and Turkey. While this grouping did highlight countries with substantial national economies, it was an assortment of nations that, upon closer inspection, had little in common beyond the relative sizes of their respective economies.

The MINT acronym, like its predecessor BRIC, garnered attention and fueled discussions about the potential of these economies. However, it also raised questions about the validity of such groupings when they encompassed countries with vastly different cultural backgrounds, geographic locations, and political landscapes. The MINT example serves as a reminder of the inherent complexities in trying to draw neat lines around groups of nations based solely on economic indicators, without taking into account the rich tapestry of factors that shape their individual identities and challenges.

In many ways, the countries comprising the BRIC grouping were markedly different from their current incarnations at the time when the initial BRIC report emerged. This report was undeniably shaped by the optimism that characterised the post-Cold War world, a time when the forces of capitalism and emerging globalisation stood prominently above all others on the global stage. It marked a transformative period in which nations like India, Russia, and China were shedding their former economic identities, emerging from self-imposed economic isolationism, and navigating the challenges of a rapidly changing global landscape.

Russia, for instance, was grappling with the aftermath of the dissolution of the Soviet Union, facing the daunting spectre of post-Soviet inflation. India, too, was in the process of opening up its markets and transitioning away from protectionist policies that had been the hallmark of its economic approach for decades. Meanwhile, China was undergoing a remarkable economic transformation, gradually shifting from a state-controlled economy to one that was increasingly integrated into the global economic order.

These nations were in the throes of profound change, and the initial BRIC report recognized the immense potential inherent in their transitions. It foresaw the emergence of these nations as significant players on the global economic stage, driven by their newfound openness to global trade and the opportunities presented by a more interconnected world.

The BRIC report thus captured a pivotal moment in history, a juncture when these countries were shedding their old economic skin and embarking on the path to becoming major economic powerhouses. It serves as a testament to the dynamic nature of global economic forces and the transformative impact of globalisation on the economic destinies of nations.

Despite the initial optimism surrounding the possibility of forming a robust multinational economic alliance among the "big 4" BRIC countries, there were underlying issues simmering just beneath the surface. These issues periodically resurfaced, casting doubt on the cohesion and long-term viability of the group following its official formation. Such doubts often centred around the intricate web of each member's strategic and geopolitical interests, which added layers of complexity to the BRIC alliance.

These complexities and challenges, which will be explored in greater detail in subsequent chapters, underscore the nuanced nature of international relations. The BRIC alliance, while founded on shared economic potential, found itself navigating a maze of divergent national interests, regional dynamics, and historical legacies. These factors, at times, brought into question the unity of the group and the ability to effectively leverage their collective strength on the global stage.

CHAPTER 2

The First BRIC

Intrigued and deeply inspired by the original Goldman Sachs report authored by Jim O'Neil, which had identified them as the "big 4" emerging economies, the foreign ministers of Brazil, Russia, India, and China embarked on a pivotal journey. In September 2006, on the margins of the General Debate of the 61st session of the UN Assembly held in New York City, these nations convened to engage in earnest discussions about the feasibility and potential of formalising the BRIC grouping into an official organisation.

This momentous meeting marked the inception of a series of high-level discussions and negotiations, all centred around the realisation of this nascent economic alliance. The foreign ministers recognized the shared economic potential and the strategic importance of their collective cooperation on the global stage. These initial deliberations set in motion a process that would culminate in the eventual establishment of a formalised organisation known as BRIC, something of a precursor to the current-day BRICS.

It is important to emphasise that this undertaking was not solely motivated by purely altruistic ideals of mutual benefit. Instead, it was heavily influenced by the geopolitical self-interests of the member nations and, in some cases, underscored underlying rivalries among notable members of the "big 4."

While the initial discussions about forming an official organisation like BRIC were rooted in the recognition of shared economic potential, it is evident that geopolitical considerations played a significant role. Each member nation had its own strategic objectives and priorities, and these sometimes divergent interests could not be ignored. The geopolitical landscape was marked by complex interplay of influence, power dynamics, and regional ambitions, all of which shaped the way these countries approached the BRIC alliance.

This intricate web of motivations and rivalries adds depth to the story of BRIC, highlighting the multifaceted nature of international diplomacy and cooperation. While mutual benefit was undoubtedly a driving force, the realities of geopolitics and national interests also loomed large in the formation and evolution of the BRIC organisation.

The inaugural formal summit of the newly established BRIC organisation marked a historic moment in international relations. This summit convened on 16 June 2009 in the city of Yekaterinburg, Russia, bringing together the heads of state from all four participating nations. It was a watershed event that solidified the organisation's status on the global stage.

The formalisation of this organisation, however, was not an isolated development. It was significantly catalysed by the 2007–2008 global financial crisis, which sent shockwaves throughout the global economy. The aftermath of this economic crisis, characterised by a multitude of issues including rising global prices and economic instability, underscored the need for emerging economies to band together and coordinate their responses to the challenges posed by an increasingly interconnected world.

The BRIC summit in Yekaterinburg represented a proactive

response to the evolving global economic landscape. It served as a platform for these nations to not only discuss their shared interests but also to collectively address the pressing issues stemming from the financial crisis. This gathering of leaders marked the official entry of BRIC onto the world stage as a powerful economic bloc, signalling its intent to play a significant role in shaping the global economic and political order.

It is indeed worth noting that Russia assumed the role of the de-facto leader within the newly formed BRIC economic pact. The available evidence strongly suggests that the Russian government was among the most enthusiastic proponents of the BRIC alliance. This enthusiasm on Russia's part can be speculated to have been driven by several factors, including a desire to reclaim their perceived glorious Soviet past when they were considered a major superpower.

The memories of Soviet-era superpower status likely fueled Russia's eagerness to assert itself on the global stage once more. The emergence of BRIC provided a strategic opportunity for Russia to position itself as a prominent player in international affairs. The timing was also significant, as it coincided with the immediate years after the U.S. subprime mortgage crisis, which created a rare instance of American vulnerability and economic uncertainty. This vulnerability could potentially be exploited by creating a rival organisation to the existing G8 structure, wherein Russia sought to elevate the BRIC alliance as a counterbalance and potential rival to Western-dominated economic and political forums. Russia's active role in the formation and leadership of BRIC underscored its determination to regain a central position in global geopolitics and economics.

In contrast to Russia's assertive leadership in the BRIC alliance, the People's Republic of China initially assumed a somewhat less active leadership role within the organisation. Over time, China's role evolved into that of a financial backer and major contributor to the BRIC organisation's initiatives. This shift in approach can be speculated to be influenced by a variety of factors, including the strategic calculations of the Chinese Communist Party (CCP) leadership.

One key consideration could have been China's perception of the BRIC alliance as a method to contain the influence of its fellow BRIC member and long-term rival, the Republic of India. The complex relationship between India and China has been marked by historical tensions, including several unresolved border disputes, a bloody conflict in 1962, and frequent armed border skirmishes. Given this context, it's possible that China saw the BRIC platform as a means to engage with India within a controlled diplomatic framework while maintaining a more dominant balance of power.

Indeed, it's a perceptive observation. Much like Russia, the Chinese leadership could have viewed the BRIC group as a potential avenue through which they could challenge the U.S.-led economic dominance on the global stage. The emergence of BRIC provided China with a strategic platform to diversify its economic and diplomatic relationships beyond the Western-dominated structures, thereby reducing its reliance on U.S.-led institutions.

China's active involvement in BRIC could have been seen as a means to foster a more Sino-centric world order, where Chinese interests play a greater role in shaping international economic policies and decisions. By participating in BRIC, China could assert its influence in efforts to reform global financial institutions like the International Monetary Fund (IMF) and the World Bank, advocating for a more equitable distribution of voting rights and decision-making authority.

The BRIC platform allowed China to align itself with other major emerging economies, amplifying its collective voice in challenging the traditional Western dominated economic order.

In this sense, BRIC served as a potential vehicle for China to strongly advocate for its interests and exert greater influence in shaping the rules of the global economic game.

It can also be observed that both Chinese and Russian leadership might have initially perceived the newly-formed BRIC bloc as a more economically-aligned extension of the existing structure, the Shanghai Cooperation Organisation (SCO) a Eurasian political, economic, international security and defence organisation, which they jointly dominate. This vision of BRIC as an economic complement to the SCO, with a focus on shared economic interests, laid the foundation for a deeper strategic partnership among these emerging powers.

Furthermore, the BRIC bloc could have been seen as an additional tool for the Chinese leadership to effectively manage the influence of regional rivals, such as India. Notably, India also holds membership in the SCO, making the interplay between BRIC and SCO a dynamic arena for regional diplomacy and influence.

From a Russian perspective, the creation of the BRIC bloc could have served as another means to align India with a more Russia-centric global vision. By fostering economic cooperation and shared interests within BRIC, Russia aimed to strengthen its ties with India, particularly during a period when India was actively seeking to diversify its international partnerships.

Traditionally, Brazil had been more aligned with its North American partner, the United States. However, the Brazilian leadership recognized substantial economic benefits in joining the BRIC bloc. Beyond the immediate economic advantages, this alliance presented Brazil with a valuable option for diversifying its economic partnerships.

The Brazilian leadership also viewed BRIC as a forum through which they could advocate for increased representation in international organisations, such as the United Nations Security

Council and other influential global bodies. Brazil, as a rising economic power with a sizable population and vast resources, aspired to play a more prominent role in shaping global governance and decision-making. By aligning with other emerging economies in BRIC, Brazil saw an opportunity to amplify its voice on the world stage, advocating for a more equitable distribution of power and representation in international institutions.

The decision to join BRIC was thus driven by a strategic calculation on Brazil's part, recognizing that this alliance offered not only economic diversification but also a platform to advance its global diplomatic objectives and assert itself as a key player in shaping the evolving global order.

India's official entrance into the newly formed BRIC bloc likely stemmed from a strategic diplomatic perspective. New Delhi, much like their Brazilian counterparts, might have viewed this emerging economic alliance as an invaluable platform to advocate for a more active and influential role in established international institutions, foremost among them being the United Nations Security Council. India, as a rapidly growing economic and political power with a significant population, aspired to have a stronger voice in shaping global governance and decision-making.

Furthermore, it can be speculated that the Indian elected leadership, driven by optimism and a forward-looking approach, considered the BRIC alliance as a potential method to address long-standing border disputes and frequent violent skirmishes, notably with China and Pakistan. Engaging within BRIC could provide a structured diplomatic framework for managing these regional tensions and conflicts.

In addition to addressing security concerns, the Indian leadership would have perceived BRIC membership as a means to enhance the country's diplomatic standing on the world stage. Joining BRIC offered India alternative economic channels and opportunities for diversification, further strengthening its global influence and engagement. These multifaceted motivations highlight the strategic calculations that led India to become an active participant in the BRIC alliance, which ultimately evolved into the BRICS organisation with significant implications for international diplomacy and economic cooperation.

Despite the "big 4" BRIC nations having their own unique differences and occasional disputes, the formation of the BRIC alliance proceeded relatively smoothly, without any major issues. This surprising cohesion among nations with diverse backgrounds and interests was emblematic of the shared recognition of the vulnerabilities in Western economic doctrine, particularly in the wake of the 2007-2008 market crash. The leadership of BRICs saw an opportunity to consolidate their collective power and present a united front against Western interests, potentially reshaping the dynamics of global economics and geopolitics.

The aftermath of the financial crisis highlighted the fragility of the existing global economic order and underscored the potential of emerging economies. BRIC, as a grouping of major emerging powers, positioned itself as a credible alternative and counterbalance to the established Western-dominated economic institutions. The stage was set for BRIC to play a more prominent role in shaping international economic policies and challenging the status quo.

However, as time passed, the unaddressed underlying issues between its member nations and the unchecked ambitions of a few of the "big 4" began to surface, causing strains within this fragile economic alliance. These issues, which will be explored in more detail in subsequent discussions, shed light on the complexities and challenges of maintaining cohesion among nations with divergent interests and aspirations, ultimately shaping the course of BRIC's evolution into the BRICS organisation.

CHAPTER 3

BRIC + South Africa = BRICS

Following its initial formation, interest in the BRIC bloc began to gain considerable traction within the developing world. Many national governments saw BRIC as their version of the G8, and whispers of intent to join this fledgling economic alliance echoed across the global stage.

BRIC's emergence as a major player in international economics and diplomacy captured the imagination of many developing nations. It represented an alternative forum where emerging economies could have a voice, challenge Western-dominated institutions, and collectively address common challenges. As such, BRIC garnered attention not only from its member nations but also from a host of other countries aspiring to be part of this dynamic alliance.

The allure of BRIC was multifaceted. It provided a platform for developing nations to engage with major global economic players, fostering opportunities for trade, investment, and diplomatic cooperation. It also symbolised a perceived shift in the balance of power within international relations, signifying the rise of emerging economies as influential actors on the global stage.

In this context, the whispers of intent to join BRIC underscored the organisation's growing significance and appeal as a force for change in the evolving landscape of international politics and economics.

One nation that displayed significant and vocal interest in joining the BRIC bloc was the rapidly rising African economy of South Africa. Around the year 2010, this post-apartheid state had emerged as one of the most prominent economic players on the African continent. Economic indicators from that decade strongly suggested that this vibrant and mineral-rich nation would continue to experience substantial economic growth.

South Africa's aspirations to join BRIC were rooted in its desire to solidify its position as a key economic and political actor, not only within Africa but also on the global stage. The nation's post-apartheid transformation had ushered in an era of increased economic engagement and international cooperation. Joining BRIC represented an opportunity for South Africa to further enhance its diplomatic and economic ties with major emerging economies while positioning itself as a bridge between Africa and the BRIC nations.

Despite all the optimism surrounding this African economic giant, it's worth noting that Jim O'Neil, the economist who authored the original report that inspired the formation of the BRIC bloc, held reservations about South Africa's potential contribution. While South Africa was experiencing short-term economic growth and had emerged as a prominent player on the African continent, O'Neil believed that it lacked the necessary population size to add significant value to the BRIC bloc.

O'Neil's perspective was rooted in the idea that South Africa, with its relatively smaller population compared to the "big 4" BRIC nations, might struggle to assert itself and could potentially be overshadowed and dominated within the alliance. His analysis highlighted the demographic disparities among BRIC members, with Brazil, Russia, India, and China each boasting substantial populations, while South Africa's population was comparatively smaller.

It's crucial to highlight that one of the most vocal proponents of South Africa joining the BRIC union was none other than one of the "big 4" BRIC nations, the People's Republic of China. China's enthusiastic interest in expanding this economic alliance to include an African member stemmed from strategic considerations rather than altruistic motives. Many scholars have described this move as a novel form of Chinese neo-colonialism.

For China, the inclusion of South Africa in BRIC offered an opportunity to extend its influence and economic reach into the African continent, which was rich in natural resources and represented a critical growth market. The Chinese Communist Party saw this expansion as a means to directly maintain a foothold in Africa, leveraging its partnership with South Africa to access the continent's abundant and strategically important resources.

By pulling South Africa into the BRIC alliance, China could position itself to exploit the economic opportunities and natural resources that Africa had to offer. This move exemplified the complexities of international relations and strategic manoeuvring within BRIC/BRICS.

Furthermore, it's worth noting that the remaining three members of the original BRIC bloc, namely Brazil, Russia, and India, were supportive of the idea of expanding their alliance to include an African nation. They saw such an expansion as a validation of the perceived stability and strength of the alliance as a whole.

For these three BRIC members, South Africa's inclusion represented a vote of confidence in their belief in the cohesion and longevity of the BRIC alliance. It signalled that BRIC was not merely a short-lived economic forum but an enduring partnership capable of welcoming new members and adapting to evolving global dynamics. This willingness to expand demonstrated the commitment of these nations to building a diverse and influential collective of emerging economies on the world stage.

With the unanimous support and blessings of the other three members—Brazil, Russia, and India—China officially extended an invitation to South Africa to join the alliance on the 24th of December 2010, an invitation that the African nation's leadership warmly embraced. This significant development marked the transformation of the BRIC bloc into the BRICS, symbolising the addition of South Africa as a full-fledged member.

South Africa's enthusiasm and eagerness to be a part of this economic alliance were further reflected in its actions. The then President of South Africa, Jacob Zuma, actively participated in the 2011 BRICS summit held in Sanya, China, not as an observer but as a fully recognized member of the BRICS alliance. This participation underscored South Africa's commitment to leveraging its role within BRICS to advance its diplomatic and economic interests on both the African and global stages. The integration of South Africa into BRICS represented a pivotal moment in the evolution of this emerging powers coalition.

Despite the prevailing buzz about BRICS being an alliance of equals and promoting inclusivity, a significant factor couldn't be overlooked—the Chinese economy notably towered over the economies of the other four member nations. This economic disparity marked the onset of what would become a series of cracks within the alliance, eventually giving rise to whispers among scholars and political pundits. Some began to suggest that BRICS was gradually evolving into a Sino-centric alliance with intentions to counter Western democratic values and influence.

The economic predominance of China within BRICS was undeniable. Its sheer size, growth trajectory, and global economic footprint set it apart as the dominant member of the alliance. While BRICS was initially conceived as a grouping of emerging economies, China's rapid ascent on the world stage had positioned it as the de facto leader, both economically and politically, within the organisation.

As this disparity became increasingly apparent, questions arose about the extent to which BRICS could truly operate as an alliance of equals. Some observers speculated that China might utilise its position to promote a more authoritarian and illiberal approach, which could potentially conflict with the democratic values championed by the Western world. These debates marked the beginning of a complex narrative surrounding BRICS' evolving dynamics and its role on the global stage.

This gradual evolution within BRICS did not go unnoticed by Russia, often symbolised as the "sleeping bear." Russia began to view BRICS as a contingency plan in the event that its lukewarm relations with the Western world took a sour turn. It was increasingly clear that such a turn was likely, given Russia's secret ambitions to reclaim lost Soviet territories and its assertive posturing toward its Western trade partners.

Russia, having emerged from the shadows of the Soviet Union, was navigating a complex geopolitical landscape. It harboured aspirations to reestablish its influence over regions that had once been part of the Soviet bloc. Simultaneously, it found itself at odds with Western powers over various international issues, leading to strained relations, an early warning for what is to come, given Russian territorial ambitions.

In this context, BRICS began to take on added significance for Russia. It offered a potential counterbalance to Western dominance and a forum for collaboration with other major emerging economies. Russia saw BRICS as a means to diversify its diplomatic and economic relationships while providing a hedge against potential conflicts with Western partners.

CHAPTER 4

A Bank for BRICS

One of the earliest collaborative endeavours undertaken by the BRICS bloc involved an ambitious attempt to secure influence within existing international financial institutions, most notably the International Monetary Fund (IMF). This initiative, spearheaded in 2012 by Russia, which at that time held substantial gold and foreign exchange reserves, entailed offering the IMF a substantial loan of $75 billion. In exchange, the BRICS members sought greater voting rights and representation within the IMF, as well as support from other allies, particularly Russia and China.

The plan was carefully crafted to enhance the influence of BRICS and its allies within the IMF, reflecting their growing economic clout on the global stage. However, despite the apparent attractiveness of a significant cash injection, the IMF did not exhibit the expected interest in the offer. This unexpected response left the BRICS initiative to increase its influence within the IMF unfulfilled, signalling early challenges in translating the bloc's economic power into meaningful changes within established powerful international institutions.

Based on the lessons learned from their early failed expansion campaign within existing financial institutions, the five BRICS members jointly decided to embark on a more ambitious path. This pivotal decision was reached during the fifth BRICS summit, held in Durban in March 2013. The summit was marked by enthusiasm from all member nations for the establishment of a new global financial institution under the BRICS umbrella.

The envisioned institution held the promise of providing emerging powers with a platform to exert greater influence in the global financial landscape, reducing their reliance on established Western-dominated institutions like the IMF and World Bank. The potential benefits of such an institution were significant, from increased financial stability to enhanced economic cooperation among BRICS members.

However, despite the initial consensus and enthusiasm, the path to establishing this new international bank proved to be protracted and fraught with challenges. Internal bickering among member countries, particularly centred on the precise share structure and governance arrangements of the institution, emerged as a significant stumbling block. These underlying issues laid bare the diverse interests and priorities of BRICS members and led to frustrating delays in the establishment of the new financial institution.

The internal discord persisted for some time, contributing to a sense of stagnation in the efforts to create the BRICS-led international bank. It appeared that the shared vision of enhanced economic cooperation was in danger of being overshadowed by conflicting interests and disagreements.

However, a significant turning point was on the horizon during the early spring months of 2014, marked by unexpected and condemnable actions by the Russian Federation. This pivotal moment would not only impact the BRICS' efforts to establish their international bank but also have broader implications for the geopolitical landscape.

In the early months of 2014, a significant and concerning development unfolded as unmarked Russian troops, primarily composed of special operations and the FSB Spetsnaz, earned the moniker of "little green men" as they undertook an illegal annexation of Ukrainian territory, specifically the Crimea region. This marked a troubling event, as it was the first time a European country had invaded another since the conclusion of World War II.

The Russian annexation of Crimea served as a stark manifestation of Russia's unchecked ambitions, marking an audacious attempt to revive the long-dormant Soviet Union. Alternatively, it could be seen as an egotistical endeavour by President Vladimir Putin to establish himself as the new Tzar of a revitalised Russian Empire. Regardless of the underlying motivations, the annexation triggered a chain of events that plunged Ukraine into a devastating civil war.

The annexation of Crimea forced Ukraine into a state of turmoil, with Kremlin-backed separatist regions coming under the sphere of Russian influence. This development strained Ukraine's relationship with the European Union, as it diverged from the desires of many Ukrainian voters who strongly favoured closer ties with the EU.

The international community responded to Russia's actions with a series of sanctions levied against the Russian state, as well as its political and business elite, by most Western nations. These sanctions represented a significant diplomatic and economic blow to Russia, isolating it on the global stage.

In the wake of these developments, Russia began to view the BRICS bloc as a more valuable lifeline than initially presumed. The alliance provided an alternative avenue for economic cooperation and support, countering the effects of Western sanctions and offering a platform for solidarity among emerging powers. This shift in perspective would have profound implications for the BRICS organisation and its evolving role in global geopolitics and economics.

Amidst mounting pressure from Russia and with the backing of China, driven by their respective self-interests, the previously delayed plans for a "New Development Bank" regained momentum. This resurgence led to the signing of the treaty of formation in July 2014, a significant development that occurred just a few months after the Russian invasion of Crimea and the deployment of Russian proxies in Russian-backed separatist territories in Ukraine.

The treaty, outlining the establishment and operational framework of the New Development Bank, was set to come into force one year from the date of signing. This meant that the New Development Bank would be officially inaugurated in July of the following year. The timing of this move was notable, as it occurred against the backdrop of heightened geopolitical tensions and changing dynamics in the international arena.

The decision to advance with the New Development Bank reflected the determination of BRICS members, particularly Russia and China, to create a financial institution that could serve as an alternative to established Western-dominated institutions. This strategic move aimed to bolster their economic cooperation and provide a counterbalance to the influence of Western powers in the global financial system.

The funding for the New Development Bank, amounting to an impressive $100 billion, had been committed during a prior gathering of BRICS nations in September 2013, which took place in St. Petersburg. During this pivotal meeting, each member nation pledged its financial contribution to the pool, reflecting their respective economic sizes and capacities.

China, as the largest economy among the BRICS nations, committed a substantial $41 billion towards the funding of the bank. This sizable contribution underscored China's position as the major financial powerhouse within the BRICS alliance.

Brazil, India, and Russia, with their relatively smaller economies, each pledged $18 billion to the funding pool. These commitments were in line with the economic strengths and capabilities of these three BRICS members.

South Africa, the smallest economy among the BRICS nations, made a contribution of $5 billion to the fund. This amount, while relatively smaller compared to its BRICS counterparts, was representative of South Africa's economic size and its commitment to the collective objectives of the New Development Bank.

In many ways, the funding structure of the New Development Bank reinforced a perspective that had been gaining traction among analysts and observers. This perspective suggested that the BRICS bloc, initially envisioned as a multipolar economic alliance, was gradually evolving into something quite different. It appeared to be less in line with the concept of a genuine multipolar economic order and more akin to a platform through which China could assert its economic influence, potentially covering for actions of autocratic regimes within the alliance.

The significant financial commitments, particularly the substantial contribution from China, raised questions about the power dynamics within BRICS. China's dominant role within the alliance, both economically and politically, led some to speculate that BRICS was becoming a Chinese economic proxy. This perception gained strength as China leveraged its position to further its own strategic interests, including support for regimes facing international criticism.

For instance, the recent Russian military conquests in Ukraine, notably the annexation of Crimea and the support for separatist forces in eastern Ukraine, had drawn widespread condemnation from the international community. Within the BRICS context, this raised concerns that the alliance could be used to provide cover or diplomatic support for such actions.

To compensate for its substantial contribution, which amounted to over 40% of the New Development Bank's liquidity, the Chinese leadership pressed for a more significant management role within the institution. Given China's economic might and the pragmatic realities of the situation, the other four BRICS members did not possess the economic capacity or political will to mount significant objections.

As a result of these negotiations, China secured a pivotal position within the New Development Bank, including the location of its headquarters. The Chinese city of Shanghai was designated as the headquarters of the newly created financial institution. This decision underscored China's prominent role within the BRICS alliance and its influence in shaping the operational aspects of the bank.

Despite the evident uneven power dynamics that shaped the operations of the New Development Bank, a fundamental principle was upheld to maintain a sense of fairness and equality among all founding members. This principle revolved around the concept of equal shareholding in the financial institution.

In practice, this meant that each of the five founding BRICS members maintained an equal shareholding in the New Development Bank. This commitment to equal shareholding was a deliberate effort to project an illusion of fairness and equality within the bank's governance structure.

In a significant development, the ownership structure of the New Development Bank witnessed the inclusion of three new members in late 2021. These newcomers were the United Arab Emirates, Bangladesh, and Egypt, signalling a growing interest among developing nations in becoming part of this alternative financing body.

The decision to expand the membership of the New Development Bank was a notable step, reflecting the institution's increasing prominence and appeal in the global financial landscape. These three new members, while joining the ranks of the existing BRICS ownership structure, were granted minority stakes in the bank.

This expansion marked a noteworthy evolution in the New Development Bank's journey, as it began to attract interest and participation from nations beyond the original BRICS alliance. It highlighted the institution's growing role as a platform for cooperation in development financing and its appeal as an alternative to established Western-dominated financial institutions.

While it was not the New Development Bank's original objective, it gradually evolved into a financier for various regimes, including autocratic governments and entities that Western financial institutions viewed as too risky or ethically questionable to finance. This unintended transformation raised important questions about the bank's role and impact in the global financial landscape.

One notable aspect of the New Development Bank's evolving role was its provision of financial support to regimes and projects that had faced scepticism or rejection from Western institutions due to concerns about risk or ethical considerations. This shift in focus gave rise to a public perception that the bank was becoming a source of funding for autocratic regimes and controversial projects.

The bank's role as a lifeline to a sanctioned Russian regime, particularly in the aftermath of the annexation of Crimea and other international disputes, further fueled this perception. Additionally, the fact that the New Development Bank was led by the People's Republic of China, a regime with a substantial list of human rights violations and a history of territorial disputes and tensions with many of its neighbours, did little to change this public perception.

The evolving nature of the New Development Bank's operations raised complex questions about its responsibilities, ethics, and the potential impact on global geopolitics. It also highlighted the challenges faced by emerging powers as they sought to balance their economic interests with their diplomatic responsibilities in the international arena.

CHAPTER 5

Sports in BRICS

While the BRICS alliance originally coalesced to nurture economic cooperation among its member nations (Brazil, Russia, India, China, and South Africa), the introduction of the BRICS Games signifies a broader dedication to enriching cultural exchanges and fostering people-to-people connections. These games serve as a platform where athletes from diverse backgrounds converge, not only to compete but also to celebrate the rich tapestry of cultures that define the BRICS nations.

The inaugural BRICS Games held in the picturesque coastal city of Goa symbolised the alliance's aspiration to merge sport with the ethos of unity and friendship. Goa, with its stunning beaches and vibrant cultural heritage, provided an ideal backdrop for projecting the image of a harmonious and culturally diverse alliance.

It's noteworthy that among the five BRICS member nations, China and Russia have historically dominated international sports tournaments, most notably the Olympics. This supremacy can be traced, in part, to their Cold War-era communist heritage and the indomitable competitive spirit that accompanies it.

China, with its vast population and robust state-sponsored sports programs, has consistently emerged as a formidable force in the world of sports. Its commitment to sporting excellence is deeply ingrained in its history, as the country's leaders have regarded athletic success as a source of national pride and soft power projection.

Similarly, Russia, under various incarnations, boasts a storied history of sporting achievement dating back to the days of the Soviet Union. The legacy of extensive state support for sports and a culture that places a premium on athletic accomplishment continue to shape Russia's desire to excel in various sporting disciplines.

This stark contrast in sporting prowess within the BRICS alliance underscores the diverse trajectories and influences that have shaped the athletic landscapes of each member nation. While China and Russia carry forward the legacy of their Cold War-era sporting might, other BRICS countries are increasingly investing in sports infrastructure and talent development, striving to make their mark on the international stage.

Amidst the global coronavirus pandemic, China adapted to the new normal by hosting the 2022 BRICS Games online. This innovative approach allowed the BRICS nations to maintain their tradition of friendly competition and cultural exchange despite the challenges posed by the global health crisis.

In defiance of global condemnation and its pariah status on the international stage, largely due to its ongoing aggressive campaign to erase an independent Ukraine from the map and erode its cultural identity, Russia is slated to host the 2024 edition of the BRICS Games. This decision raises significant ethical and political concerns, given Russia's persistent disregard for international norms and its continued isolation from the global community.

Russia's actions in Ukraine have not only destabilised Eastern Europe but also strained diplomatic relations on a global scale. Its expansionist policies, which have resulted in the suffering of innocent civilians and the violation of Ukraine's sovereignty, have garnered resounding condemnation from democratic nations.

Against this grim backdrop, the decision to entrust Russia with the hosting of the 2024 BRICS Games sends a disconcerting message about the alliance's priorities. While the BRICS member nations initially came together for economic cooperation, the decision to overlook Russia's actions in Ukraine undermines the alliance's credibility and raises profound questions about its commitment to human rights, democracy, and international law.

It is incumbent upon the BRICS nations to critically evaluate their choice of host country for the BRICS Games and carefully consider the ethical implications of their decisions. Sporting events should stand as beacons of peace, cooperation, and respect for human rights, rather than platforms that inadvertently legitimise regimes that float these principles on the global stage.

As the world watches, the 2024 BRICS Games in Russia will not only be a test of athletic prowess but also a litmus test for the alliance's dedication to upholding the principles of international law and justice, even in the face of formidable geopolitical challenges.

CHAPTER 6

An optical cable that never was

One of the most ambitious infrastructure projects ever proposed within the BRICS alliance, the BRICS cable, ultimately met a grim fate, never seeing the light of day. Originally introduced in 2012, this visionary underwater optical cable project aimed to forge a direct, independent network connecting all BRICS nations and their regional partners, circumventing the grip of established Western players over global telecommunications.

This audacious undertaking was driven by a resurgence of nationalistic fervour within BRICS member nations, fueled by an international outcry triggered by the damning revelations of extensive global surveillance operations orchestrated by Western intelligence agencies. These disclosures unmasked various mass surveillance initiatives led by the United States Intelligence community and their secretive "Five Eyes" allies, which included the United States, the United Kingdom, Canada, Australia, and New Zealand.

The BRICS cable project boasted ambitious plans for its initial landing points, strategically situated across member nations. These locations encompass Fortaleza (Brazil), Cape Town (South Africa), Mauritius, Chennai (India), Singapore, Shantou (China), and Vladivostok (Russia). Each point was meticulously chosen to facilitate seamless connectivity and communication among BRICS nations and their regional partners.

It's worth noting that the government of Brazil emerged as one of the most ardent champions of this endeavour, reflecting Brazil's deep commitment to enhancing regional and international cooperation within the BRICS framework. The project was perceived as an avenue to fortify Brazil's connectivity and assert its pivotal role in the alliance.

However, despite the initial enthusiasm and the urgency ignited by concerns over privacy and national sovereignty, there has been a deafening silence surrounding the BRICS cable project since 2015. As of 2023, it is widely assumed that little, if any, substantive progress has been made, with the initial infrastructure developments likely abandoned in disrepair.

The foremost factor contributing to the project's abandonment likely stems from economic impracticality. This grandiose, intricate endeavour, known as the BRICS cable, was projected to cost upwards of $185 million—a figure once touted by BRICS leadership. This substantial cost presented formidable financial hurdles, ultimately eclipsing the anticipated benefits of the project.

Ironically, the decision to let the BRICS cable project languish may have been a blessing in disguise. Even though it was born from concerns about the actions of the United States and its allies, its realisation could have ushered in a litany of new worries. It would have afforded Russian and Chinese intelligence agencies nearly boundless resources and opportunities to surveil the communications of individuals in nations connected to the BRICS cable, all with minimal oversight.

It's imperative to emphasise that both Russia and China, as BRICS members, have cultivated reputations for employing repressive tactics against individuals who dare to criticise or oppose the interests of their ruling elites. The potential for abuse and violations of privacy in such a scenario would have been a grave concern, raising ethical and security issues with far-reaching implications for every citizen in a nation connected to the hypothetical BRICS cable.

Despite this monumental setback and the practical implausibility of the BRICS cable ever materialising, a disquieting silence lingers. There is a conspicuous absence of any official updates or statements from either the BRICS organisation or its member states regarding the project's formal cancellation. This unsettling silence hints at the possibility, however remote, that the alliance clings to the fragile hope of reviving the project at some indeterminate point in the future.

This ominous lack of closure underscores the enduring ambiguities surrounding the BRICS cable. While the project faced insurmountable hurdles and was fraught with economic impracticality from its inception, the alliance's persistent refusal to officially abandon it speaks to a certain stubbornness or reluctance to accept the project's inevitable demise.

In truth, the prospects of the BRICS cable ever becoming a reality remain distant, obscured by the harsh realities of geopolitics, strained economic conditions, and the formidable challenges that originally brought about its downfall. The collective silence from BRICS member states may serve as a testament to their shared hesitation to acknowledge the project's grim fate.

The saga of the BRICS cable stands as a stark reminder of how even the most grandiose ambitions can crumble in the face of insurmountable pragmatic constraints. It stands as a symbol of unfulfilled aspirations within an alliance that, despite its lofty ideals and objectives, often grapples with the unforgiving realities of international politics and economics.

CHAPTER 7

United in Statistics

One of the lesser-known but relatively successful initiatives within the BRICS bloc is the annual joint publication by the IBGE representing Brazil, Rosstat from Russia, the National Bureau of Statistics of China, the Central Statistics Office of India, and Statistics South Africa. First introduced in 2011, this collaborative endeavour holds a unique position within the BRICS alliance, fostering cooperation in the realm of statistical data and analysis.

The primary focus of this annual report is to provide a comprehensive perspective on statistical production. It goes beyond mere data sharing to delve into the intricate details of methodologies adopted by each participating nation. This approach allows for a deeper understanding of how statistical results are generated and the factors that may influence variations in data interpretation.

One of the central objectives of this publication is to facilitate comparative analysis. By presenting statistical results side by side, it becomes possible to identify commonalities, disparities, and trends across the BRICS countries. This, in turn, enables policymakers, researchers, and economists to make informed decisions based on a broader, more nuanced understanding of the economic, social, and demographic landscapes within the alliance.

The significance of this joint publication extends beyond statistical harmonisation. It serves as a vital tool for enhancing transparency and accountability in each member nation's statistical practices. By subjecting their methodologies and outcomes to scrutiny within the BRICS framework, participating countries not only demonstrate their commitment to data integrity but also gain valuable insights into best practices and areas for improvement.

Furthermore, this publication embodies the BRICS spirit of cooperation and mutual benefit. It fosters a sense of camaraderie among member nations, emphasising the idea that collaboration, even in the seemingly technical realm of statistics, can yield tangible benefits for all involved. By pooling their resources and expertise, BRICS countries amplify their collective voice on the global stage.

While this initiative may not garner the same level of attention as high-profile BRICS summits or economic agreements, its impact should not be underestimated. It exemplifies the alliance's original commitment to multifaceted cooperation, extending beyond economics to the realm of data-driven decision-making. In an era where accurate and reliable data is essential for informed governance and policy formulation, the BRICS joint publication on statistical analysis stands as a testament to the alliance's potential for forward-thinking approach and commitment to mutual progress.

CHAPTER 8

Unnecessary Baggage
of a Paper Bear

The Russian Federation's evolving role within BRICS serves as a stark reminder of how geopolitical actions and policies can profoundly impact the dynamics of international alliances. It underscores the challenges faced by BRICS in maintaining unity while addressing the behaviour of a member state that deviates significantly from the alliance's stated founding principles and goals.

Additionally, the economic repercussions of Russia's actions have been keenly felt within the BRICS bloc. The imposition of sanctions by Western nations in response to Russia's actions in Ukraine and Syria has had a ripple effect on the economies of its fellow BRICS members. The disruption of trade and economic cooperation, coupled with the instability caused by geopolitical tensions, has hindered the alliance's ability to achieve its original economic objectives.

Furthermore, Russia's assertive foreign policy and its disregard for international norms have strained its relations not only with Western countries but also with its fellow BRICS members. The alliance, which was envisioned as a platform for cooperation and dialogue, has found itself grappling with internal divisions caused by Russia's actions. Member states with different values and approaches to international affairs are now navigating the delicate task of balancing their partnership within BRICS with their broader foreign policy objectives.

The situation is further complicated by Russia's continued provocations and its willingness to use its perceived military might as a tool of intimidation. The regular threats of using its vast nuclear stockpile against perceived enemies have not only alarmed the international community but have also put pressure on the rest of the BRICS alliance to respond to such rhetoric.

Moreover, the illegal occupation of Ukrainian territories and allegations of attempted genocide against the Ukrainian people have escalated tensions to a critical point. The rest of the BRICS members now find themselves in a position where they are compelled to take a stance against such actions to uphold the principles of international law and human rights, even if it means distancing themselves from a fellow member.

It is important to acknowledge that the militaristic and expansionist nature of the Russian Federation predates its involvement in the BRICS bloc. Instances of this expansionist tendency can be traced back to events such as the conflict in Georgia, the situation in Moldova, and, to a lesser extent, the regions within Russia itself, such as Chechnya and Dagestan.

Before Russia's participation in BRICS, it had already been involved in geopolitical actions that raised concerns among the international community. The conflict in Georgia, particularly the Russo-Georgian War of 2008, marked a significant moment when Russian military forces intervened in Georgia's territory, leading to a protracted dispute over regions like South Ossetia and Abkhazia.

Similarly, in Moldova, the issue of Transnistria and Russia's involvement in the region had been a long-standing concern.

The presence of Russian troops and support for separatist movements complicated the Moldovan conflict and contributed to regional instability.

Within Russia itself, the conflicts in Chechnya and Dagestan showcased the Kremlin's willingness to use military force to suppress separatist movements and maintain control over restive regions.

In this evolving landscape, the BRICS alliance faces the daunting task of recalibrating its objectives and strategies. It must address the challenge of balancing economic interests with ethical considerations, and it must navigate the complexities of international relations in an era marked by geopolitical tensions and assertive powers.

The Russian Federation's transformation from a leader within BRICS to a source of division and concern serves as a stark reminder of the fragility of international alliances and the need for shared values and principles to sustain such partnerships. As BRICS continues to adapt to this changing reality, it faces a defining moment in its history, one that will test its ability to remain a cohesive and effective alliance in an ever-shifting global landscape.

Apart from the destroyed political image, the perceived image of a sleeping bear for the post-Soviet state's military has been unmasked for what it is: barely a paper bear, propped up by a corrupt regime to scare off potential perceived enemies. Recent actions by the Ukrainian defenders have exposed this facade for the world to see.

These recent series of military defeats at the hands of what the Russian regime once described as a weak Ukrainian lie has put a major spotlight on the levels of corruption prevalent on all levels of Russian governmental and private institutes. Power has been centralised with an elite few, including oligarchs and the siloviki —the political elites from military and intelligence backgrounds who act as sycophants for President Putin's delusions of grandeur and conquest.

The notion of a formidable Russian military, a relic of its Soviet-era might, has been shattered by the realities on the ground. What was once portrayed as a powerful and efficient military machine has been exposed as riddled with inefficiencies, outdated equipment, and demoralisation. The inability to achieve strategic objectives in Ukraine and the heavy toll inflicted by Ukrainian defenders have eroded the international perception of Russia's military prowess.

The Russian military losses in Ukraine have far-reaching and long-standing effects that extend beyond the battlefield, significantly impacting the nation's production capabilities. Coupled with the recent series of sanctions imposed by the international community, the Russian economy finds itself in a state of near-collapse.

The toll on Russia's military infrastructure has been devastating. The loss of equipment, manpower, and resources has strained the country's ability to maintain and modernise its armed forces. Repairing or replacing damaged and destroyed hardware has proven to be an immense financial burden, further exacerbating the economic challenges Russia faces.

The consequences of these military losses have rippled through the broader economy. Russia's defence industry, once a cornerstone of its manufacturing sector, now struggles to meet its commitments. The diversion of resources to the military has squeezed other sectors, leading to shortages and disruptions in essential supply chains.

The international sanctions imposed in response to Russia's actions in Ukraine have compounded these economic woes. These sanctions, which target key sectors of the Russian economy, including energy, finance, and technology, have isolated Russia from global markets. International companies have withdrawn investments, and foreign trade has plummeted.

The devaluation of the Russian ruble, coupled with soaring inflation, has eroded the purchasing power of ordinary citizens. The Russian government's attempts to stabilise the economy through capital controls and currency interventions have had limited success, exacerbating economic uncertainty.

Moreover, the flight of human capital and a brain drain of skilled professionals, entrepreneurs, and innovators has further hampered Russia's economic prospects. The allure of more stable and open economies abroad has drawn talent away from Russia, leaving a void in critical sectors.

As a result, the Russian economy finds itself in a state of crisis, grappling with economic contraction, dwindling reserves, and rising social discontent. The nation's economic woes are not solely the result of external sanctions but also a reflection of systemic issues, including corruption, lack of diversification, and an overreliance on energy exports.

The Russian government faces a daunting challenge in addressing these economic hardships while simultaneously dealing with the ongoing military conflict in Ukraine. It must make difficult choices regarding resource allocation and economic reform to stabilise the nation's finances and foster long-term economic growth.

This revelation has had far-reaching implications for Russia's political leadership. The centralization of power in the hands of a select few oligarchs and siloviki has come under scrutiny, revealing a system characterised by cronyism and corruption. The military failures have exposed not only the limitations of Russia's armed forces but also the lack of accountability and transparency within its government and military institutions.

President Putin's delusions of grandeur and conquest, once bolstered by the perception of a strong military, now face a harsh reality check. The international community has witnessed the consequences of aggressive expansionist policies and the costs incurred by the Russian people in terms of lives lost and economic sanctions.

The ongoing conflict in Ukraine has laid bare the stark contrast between the Kremlin's rhetoric and the true state of affairs in Russia. It has highlighted the urgent need for reform, both within its military and governance structures, to address the systemic issues that have undermined the country's capabilities on the world stage.

As Russia grapples with the fallout of its military failures and the international isolation resulting from its actions, questions arise about the country's future trajectory. Will it continue down a path of aggression and isolation, or will it heed the lessons of its recent defeats and embark on a path of reform and reintegration into the international community?

The recent spotlight on corruption, inefficiency, and military inadequacies within Russia serves as a sobering reminder of the challenges facing the nation. It underscores the importance of transparent governance, accountability, and responsible international behaviour in an increasingly interconnected world.

Identifying considerable weakness in the current Russian leadership, the Chinese leadership has initiated what could be described as a silent coup against the existing unofficial leadership structure that once formed the bedrock of the BRICS bloc. This manoeuvre has been facilitated by the economic vulnerability of Russia, a consequence of the severe international sanctions imposed on the country. As of the time of writing, Russia has become increasingly dependent on Chinese trade, which has given the Chinese Communist Party a substantial advantage in shaping the dynamics within BRICS.

The Chinese leadership's strategic approach reflects its growing influence and ambitions on the global stage. China's economic prowess and its ability to weather international economic storms have allowed it to assert itself within BRICS with relative ease. The economic disparity between a crippled Russia and a resilient China has shifted the balance of power within the alliance.

One significant development in this evolving landscape is Russia's pursuit of closer trade relations with another pariah state: the ironically named Democratic People's Republic of Korea, commonly known as North Korea. This nation, sustained by a Chinese lifeline, has become another piece in the puzzle of China's expanding influence.

China's adept manoeuvring within the BRICS framework, combined with its strategic economic partnerships, has enabled it to challenge the previous leadership hierarchy and potentially reshape the alliance's priorities and objectives. This subtle shift of influence underscores the fluidity of international alliances and the ability of emerging powers to seize opportunities in a rapidly changing global order.

The BRICS alliance, once seen as a coalition of equals, now grapples with the complexities of power dynamics within its ranks. As China rises as a dominant force, the future of BRICS becomes increasingly intertwined with China's economic, political, and strategic interests.

For its part, India has conspicuously refrained from condemning Russia's actions and war crimes in Ukraine, a stance that has raised eyebrows on the international stage. Rather than denouncing the ongoing conflict, India has chosen to view the economically crippled Russia as a reliable source of crude oil, indirectly contributing to the funding of Russian war efforts in Ukraine. This approach has sparked criticism and accusations of hypocrisy against India, particularly for a nation that proudly proclaims itself as the 'world's largest democracy.'

The glaring contradiction between India's democratic principles and its tacit support for the invasion of a fellow democratic state by a larger autocratic power is a stark testament to the erosion of moral values in international politics. Indian lawmakers have skillfully avoided addressing this inconsistency when questioned by the international community, displaying a cynical disregard for the principles of democracy and human rights.

This diplomatic tightrope-walking reflects India's cynical geopolitical calculations. On one hand, India seeks to maintain a strategic partnership with Russia, a historic ally and supplier of crucial defence equipment. The reliance on Russian oil plays a significant role in India's energy security, making it reluctant to sever ties with Moscow.

On the other hand, India's moral compass appears to have been discarded in favour of pragmatic interests. It values its relationships with Western democracies but is willing to overlook Russia's transgressions in Ukraine for the sake of perceived economic stability and military support.

The realpolitik considerations driving India's stance underscore the moral bankruptcy that has permeated international diplomacy. India's cynical approach seeks to safeguard its narrow national interests while turning a blind eye to the suffering and violation of democratic principles in Ukraine. This approach comes at the cost of India's moral standing on the global stage, as it willingly sacrifices its principles for short-term economic and strategic gain.

As the conflict in Ukraine continues to unfold, India's position serves as a stark reminder of the ethical compromises made by many nations in pursuit of their self-interest. The erosion of democratic values in international politics raises unsettling questions about the future of global diplomacy and the willingness of emerging powers to abandon their moral compass in the pursuit of power.

It could be speculated that the recent actions of Russia may eventually prompt the BRICS bloc to contemplate the expulsion of Russia as the international community tightens its grip on the Russian regime. The situation has escalated to the point where the International Criminal Court (ICC) has already issued a warrant against the current Russian president, Vladimir Putin, as of the time of writing.

The notion of expelling a member from a bloc initially designed for economic cooperation due to severe ethical and legal violations represents a significant turning point in the BRICS alliance's history. The bloc, formed with the vision of promoting economic growth, development, and mutual cooperation, now faces the uncomfortable reality of having one of its key members facing international criminal charges.

The ICC's issuance of a warrant against President Putin underscores the gravity of the allegations against the Russian regime. It sends a clear message to the international community that the actions of the Russian government in Ukraine are not only morally indefensible but may also constitute serious violations of international law.

This development forces the BRICS nations to confront a challenging dilemma. On one hand, they are bound by the principles of the alliance, which include non-interference in the internal affairs of member states. On the other hand, the actions of a fellow member have crossed a threshold of international norms and legal standards, raising profound ethical and practical concerns.

Expelling Russia from the BRICS bloc, if it were to occur, would represent a symbolic and consequential step. It would signify the alliance's commitment to upholding international law and human rights, even when faced with difficult decisions regarding a former ally. Such a move would demonstrate the

BRICS nations' refusal to condone or be complicit in actions that violate the principles they ostensibly stand for.

However, the path to expulsion is fraught with complexities. It requires the consensus of all BRICS member states, and any decision would have far-reaching diplomatic, economic, and geopolitical implications. Moreover, it would signal a fracture within the alliance, potentially weakening its collective bargaining power on the global stage.

The situation remains fluid, and the future of Russia's involvement in BRICS hinges on various factors, including the outcome of international investigations, legal proceedings, and the evolving dynamics within the alliance. The BRICS nations find themselves at a crossroads, facing a choice between upholding their principles or maintaining a fragile unity that risks being tainted by association with Russia's actions.

As the international community continues to respond to the crisis in Ukraine and hold those responsible to account, the BRICS bloc faces a defining moment that will shape its identity and role in the emerging global order.

The major question at the heart of the BRICS bloc's future lies in the choices its member nations will make. Will they resolutely adhere to the ethical integrity and ideals that served as the foundation for the creation of BRICS, or will they gradually drift into a pattern of hypocritical decisions? Such decisions could potentially erode the alliance's cohesiveness and ultimately lead to its isolation and fragmentation on the international stage.

The path they choose will not only define the character and purpose of the BRICS alliance but also exert a profound influence on the evolving global geopolitical landscape. It remains to be seen how these nations navigate the intricate web of international relations, balancing their commitment to shared principles with the complex realities of diplomatic and economic interests. In the face of mounting challenges, both internal and external, the collective decisions of BRICS member states will shape the destiny of this alliance and determine whether it remains a force for cooperation or succumbs to the pressures of global politics.

CHAPTER 9

Rising Dragon

As implied in the previous chapter, it's evident that the Chinese regime has consistently harboured aspirations of attaining the status of a global superpower. This ambition extends to the vision of China dominating the entire "old world" while simultaneously containing the influence of the United States within the Americas. However, it is crucial to note that the Chinese leadership does not necessarily view the BRICS bloc as an alliance of equals. Instead, they perceive it as a strategic tool to be exclusively employed against Western institutions and powers.

This perspective sheds light on the complex dynamics within the BRICS alliance, where China's ambitions and strategic calculations often shape the bloc's collective actions and priorities. It underscores the instrumental role that BRICS plays in China's broader geopolitical strategy, emphasising the alliance's significance as a means to challenge Western dominance and further China's own interests on the global stage.

The BRICS alliance, once seen as a platform for cooperation among emerging economies, takes on new dimensions in this light. It becomes a battleground of interests, where China's dominant role and strategic manoeuvres impact the alliance's direction and purpose. The tensions and intricacies within BRICS are reflective of the broader shifts in global power dynamics, where established and emerging powers vie for influence and dominance.

Moreover, the BRICS alliance can serve as a valuable instrument for the People's Republic of China in containing regional adversaries and emerging Asian powers, including Japan, Vietnam, South Korea, and even fellow BRICS member India.

One might wonder why China is so determined to assert dominance over its neighbours. To understand this, one need only examine China's historical context—a legacy marked by a series of conflicts, occupations, and what they refer to as the "century of humiliation."

The Opium Wars of the mid-19th century, initiated by the British Empire, and to a lesser extent France, resulted in China's defeat and the imposition of unequal treaties. The wars stemmed from the British desire to trade opium in China, which led to widespread addiction and social problems. While the primary actors in these wars were Western powers, Indian involvement played a notable role, particularly through the British East India Company.

The British East India Company, a powerful trading entity during the British Empire's colonial expansion, was heavily involved in the opium trade between British-controlled India and China. Indian-grown opium was a crucial commodity for the British Empire, serving as a major source of revenue. The opium was cultivated in India, primarily in the regions of Bengal and Bihar, and then shipped to China.

Indian labourers and traders played essential roles in the cultivation, processing, and transportation of opium from India to China. This trade became a significant source of wealth for the

British East India Company, as the demand for opium in China was high. Chinese authorities' efforts to curb the opium trade led to tensions and eventually the outbreak of the Opium Wars.

One of the key events that intensified the conflict was the destruction of a significant quantity of British-owned opium by Chinese officials in 1839. This event, known as the "Opium War," was a direct response to Chinese attempts to halt the opium trade. In retaliation, the British government, with Indian involvement, launched military campaigns against China, leading to the First Opium War (1839-1842) and the subsequent Treaty of Nanking.

The Treaty of Nanking, signed in 1842, marked the end of the First Opium War and resulted in significant concessions by China to Britain. These concessions included the cession of Hong Kong to British control, the opening of five treaty ports for British trade, and the payment of a substantial indemnity to Britain.

Indian labourers, particularly those from the regions involved in opium production, played crucial roles in the cultivation, processing, and transportation of opium. This direct Indian involvement in the opium trade underscores the complex and often exploitative nature of colonial economic relationships during that period.

It's important to note that while the Opium Wars and the opium trade were driven by British interests, Indian individuals and communities were significant participants in these historical events, reflecting the interconnectedness of colonial economies and their far-reaching impacts on various regions and populations.

The Chinese people also remember atrocities such as the Rape of Nanking during World War II, when Japanese forces brutally massacred Chinese civilians and soldiers, systematically raping and pillaging the city. The Rape of Nanking, also known as the Nanking Massacre, involved horrific acts of violence, including mass killings and sexual violence against the civilian population. These events, along with the broader context of foreign invasions and unequal treaties, have left a lasting impact on the Chinese psyche.

The Japanese occupation of China during World War II was marked by widespread suffering and loss of life, and the memories of these dark days continue to shape Chinese perceptions of external powers. The brutality of the Nanking Massacre, in particular, is a painful and traumatic chapter in Chinese history that is frequently invoked in discussions of foreign policy and national identity.

China's history is also marked by the Boxer Rebellion, a violent anti-foreign and anti-Christian uprising in the late 19th century, and the signing of unequal treaties that ceded territory to foreign powers. All of these historical events have contributed to China's determination to regain its position as a global power and to protect its sovereignty and territorial integrity.

The "century of humiliation" includes these events and the foreign occupation of Chinese territories. They have fostered a deep sense of national pride and a desire to restore China's position as a global power. It has also made the Chinese populace highly suspicious of foreign intentions and has been leveraged by the Chinese Communist Party to consolidate domestic support for its policies.

In light of these dynamics, it becomes apparent that the BRICS alliance holds multifaceted significance for China, serving as both a means of securing resources and a tool for regional influence and containment. However, this pursuit of dominance comes at a cost—strained relations with neighbouring nations, international criticism, and growing concerns about China's expansionist ambitions. As the BRICS bloc evolves, the world watches with a sense of apprehension, as China's assertiveness in the alliance reflects a broader shift in global power dynamics —one characterised by a rising superpower willing to challenge established norms and institutions to achieve its objectives, even if it means undermining the very principles that formed the BRICS bloc in the first place.

In a disturbing parallel, some observers have noted that the Chinese Communist state is exhibiting characteristics reminiscent of the now-defunct Japanese empire that they openly despise. There are concerning trends, including regular military clashes with neighbouring countries, strict censorship of free speech, extensive surveillance of the civilian population, cultural suppression and persecution of ethnic minorities, a crackdown on religious practices that the state deems a threat, and the existence of internment camps with eerie similarities to the infamous Soviet gulags.

The Chinese Communist Party's authoritarian approach to governance has raised international concerns about human rights abuses, particularly regarding the treatment of ethnic and religious minorities, such as the Uighurs in Xinjiang. Reports of mass detentions, forced labour, and cultural suppression have prompted outrage from the international community and calls for accountability.

The expansion of China's surveillance state, often referred to as the "Great Firewall," has led to strict control over the flow of information, stifling dissent and free expression. This control extends to social media platforms, online content, and the monitoring of individual activities, creating an environment of self-censorship and fear.

Furthermore, China's assertive territorial claims in the South China Sea and border disputes with neighbouring countries have resulted in military tensions and standoffs, raising concerns about regional stability.

The parallel with the actions of the former Japanese empire

during its imperial expansion and occupation of Asian territories during the early 20th century is a disconcerting one. It highlights the evolving nature of authoritarianism and the challenges it poses to international norms and human rights.

As the Chinese state continues to assert its dominance on the global stage, these troubling trends have far-reaching implications for regional stability and international relations. Understanding these parallels and addressing the issues they raise is of paramount importance for the international community.

The activities and policies of the Chinese state have undeniably heightened the sense of hypocrisy within the BRICS alliance. While the alliance collectively emphasises the importance of human rights, respect for sovereign territory, and democratic values, there is often a reluctance to meaningfully condemn the concerning actions of one of its own members.

This reluctance can be attributed, at least in part, to the significant power disparity within BRICS, with China standing as the largest and most powerful economy in the bloc. This economic dominance gives China considerable influence over the other four members, and this influence is widely acknowledged within the alliance. It has reached a point where China's economic might enables it to effectively veto any BRICS project or activity that it opposes.

Additionally, recent events, such as Russia's military vulnerabilities exposed in Ukraine, have shifted the dynamics within BRICS. China has emerged as the de facto military powerhouse of the alliance, further solidifying its influence and making it a formidable entity that the other BRICS members may prefer not to provoke.

This power imbalance has created a complex situation within BRICS, where the pursuit of economic cooperation and shared objectives must contend with the reality of differing values, interests, and capabilities among its members. It raises questions about the alliance's ability to maintain a unified stance on critical issues, particularly when the interests of its most powerful member come into play.

The challenge for BRICS lies in navigating these internal dynamics while upholding the principles and ideals it claims to represent. As the economic and geopolitical landscape continues to evolve, the alliance faces a pivotal test of its ability to reconcile its aspirations with the realities of its membership.

For Brazil, Russia, India, and South Africa, maintaining a cooperative relationship with China is essential for economic growth and development. Chinese investment, trade, and infrastructure projects have contributed significantly to the economic advancement of these nations. However, they are also keenly aware of the potential risks of becoming overly dependent on China, both economically and geopolitically.

India, for instance, has concerns about China's territorial claims and military assertiveness along their shared border. Brazil worries about competition in key sectors like agriculture and mining. South Africa seeks to balance its economic interests with the need to protect its national sovereignty and human rights concerns.

These complexities have made it challenging for BRICS to present a united front on critical global issues. While the alliance's founding principles revolve around fostering economic cooperation and addressing shared challenges, such as poverty and inequality, the reality is often more nuanced. The member countries must weigh their economic interests against their commitment to democratic values, human rights, and international law.

As China's influence within BRICS continues to grow, the alliance's ability to address these complexities and maintain its ethical integrity faces a critical test. The world watches closely as BRICS navigates the delicate balance between economic pragmatism and upholding the principles that brought these nations together. The decisions made in the coming years will shape the trajectory of this alliance and impact global geopolitics in significant ways.

CHAPTER 10

Brazil's Play

Brazil's unique position within the BRICS economic alliance, and its earlier incarnation as the BRIC, has consistently set it apart from some of its fellow member countries. While the BRICS alliance has gradually transformed into a formidable rival of Western institutions and interests, Brazil has adopted a measured approach, maintaining a distinct distance from the more polarising actions championed by certain nationalistic or anti-Western politicians in the alliance.

This distinctive Brazilian approach can be attributed, in part, to the nation's historical ties with the United States and other Western democracies. These long standing connections have significantly influenced Brazil's pragmatic foreign policy stance, setting it apart from the more ideologically driven positions taken by some of its BRICS counterparts.

Within the BRICS framework, Brazil's nuanced foreign policy mirrors its broader international engagement strategy. Instead of embracing confrontational positions, Brazil has consistently pursued a path characterised by diplomatic flexibility and a strong commitment to multilateralism.

A noteworthy period in this diplomatic trajectory was during the presidency of Luiz Inácio Lula da Silva from 2003 to 2010.

Brazil actively sought to leverage the BRICS platform to advance its economic interests and promote South-South cooperation. Simultaneously, it engaged constructively with Western powers, including the United States and the European Union, on various global issues. This approach allowed Brazil to skillfully navigate the complex web of international power centres while safeguarding its sovereignty and pursuing its national interests as a member of the BRICS alliance. It stands as a testament to Brazil's role as a responsible and constructive global actor with a pragmatic foreign policy orientation.

Furthermore, Brazil's relatively moderate stance within BRICS aligns with its broader aspirations of being recognized as a regional leader and a global player. The nation has actively sought to strike a balance between its commitment to the principles of multipolarity and the promotion of global governance reforms on one hand, and its steadfast adherence to democratic values, human rights, and international law on the other.

In essence, Brazil's positioning within BRICS underscores its willingness to engage in dialogue and cooperation, even with nations that may have differing ideologies or political orientations. This pragmatic approach has enabled Brazil to harness the economic opportunities presented by the BRICS alliance while preserving its core values and safeguarding its interests on the international stage. Brazil's adept navigation of the complex landscape of global and regional geopolitics sets it apart as a distinctive member of the BRICS economic alliance.

However, it is crucial to acknowledge that Brazil's participation in the BRICS alliance carries certain risks, particularly concerning the country's internal dynamics and foreign policy orientation. One potential pitfall lies in how certain member states of the BRICS bloc may inadvertently contribute to Brazil's more authoritarian tendencies.

Within the BRICS framework, some member states may unintentionally bolster elements within the Brazilian government that lean toward a more authoritarian approach. These elements may harbour aspirations of returning to the military dictatorship that once characterised Brazil's political landscape. While the BRICS alliance primarily focuses on economic cooperation and development, its members may, on occasion, offer diplomatic support that goes beyond economic matters.

This diplomatic support, while well-intentioned in terms of fostering unity and solidarity within the BRICS bloc, can inadvertently embolden and validate authoritarian elements within member states, including Brazil. It may serve as a platform for the exchange of ideas and strategies, potentially contributing to the entrenchment of authoritarian tendencies in some cases.

Brazil's history bears witness to a tumultuous period of military dictatorship that endured from 1964 to 1985. During this dark chapter, the Brazilian government fell under the control of the military following a coup d'état. The military justified its actions by citing the need to maintain order and stability in the face of perceived threats from communism and social unrest.

Under the military regime, Brazil experienced a significant erosion of civil liberties and democratic institutions. Political opponents, activists, and dissidents were subjected to censorship, surveillance, and persecution. Torture and arbitrary arrests became widespread, and many individuals "disappeared" under mysterious circumstances.

One of the most notorious episodes of this era was the enactment of "AI-5" (Institutional Act Number Five) in 1968. This act granted the government sweeping powers to suppress dissent, dissolve political parties, and impose censorship on the media. It marked a pivotal moment in the authoritarian rule of the military junta and ushered in a period of intensified repression.

Economically, the military dictatorship pursued state-led development and industrialization policies. While these strategies did lead to some economic growth, they also exacerbated social inequalities and contributed to environmental degradation. The economic gains of this period came at a significant cost in terms of human rights and democratic freedoms.

It wasn't until the mid-1980s that Brazil embarked on a transition back to civilian rule, with the military gradually ceding power. The return to democracy was characterised by significant political reforms, including the drafting of a new constitution in 1988.

The memories of the military dictatorship continue to cast a long shadow over Brazilian society and politics. The nation's commitment to democracy and the protection of human rights is deeply rooted in the collective memory of this authoritarian past. As Brazil navigates its role within the BRICS alliance and the complexities of international diplomacy, these historical experiences serve as a poignant reminder of the paramount importance of upholding democratic values and respecting human rights in both domestic and international affairs.

Furthermore, the BRICS alliance does offer financial opportunities that can be advantageous for Brazil. Nevertheless, it is important to acknowledge that these financial avenues may come with less stringent requirements concerning human rights and the control of high levels of corruption. While economic cooperation stands as a central pillar of the BRICS alliance, there is an imperative for member states to balance economic interests with the promotion of democratic values, human rights, and good governance.

In this context, Brazil must exercise caution to ensure that its engagement with the BRICS alliance does not compromise its commitment to democratic principles and human rights. The nation's historical struggle with authoritarianism underscores the importance of upholding these values while pursuing economic opportunities within the alliance.

Ultimately, Brazil's participation in BRICS represents a delicate balancing act, where economic interests must align with the preservation of democratic norms and institutions. By effectively navigating this balance, Brazil can maximise the benefits of its involvement in the BRICS alliance while steadfastly upholding its commitment to democratic governance and human rights.

It is worth noting that the only BRICS initiative in which Brazil has taken a somewhat active or leadership role to date is the now-abandoned BRICS cable project, as mentioned in a previous chapter. Speculation, supported by circumstantial evidence, suggests that Brazil's vocal support for such a vast project may have been less about a long-term commitment to such an infrastructure endeavour and more about a vocal objection to the US-led global surveillance project run by the National Security Agency (NSA), which encompassed unsuspecting Brazilian civilians.

Brazil's involvement in the BRICS cable project can be viewed through the lens of both economic and geopolitical considerations. On the economic front, the initiative aimed to create a high-capacity undersea cable system connecting the BRICS nations, which would have significantly bolstered internet connectivity and data transfer capabilities within the alliance. This, in turn, could have driven economic growth and technological advancement among the member countries.

However, it's essential to consider the broader geopolitical context in which Brazil's support for this initiative unfolded. The revelations made by Edward Snowden, a former NSA contractor, regarding extensive surveillance activities by the NSA, including the monitoring of global communications and the interception of data from various countries, sent shockwaves across the international community.

Brazil, in particular, was deeply concerned about the extent of the NSA's surveillance activities within its borders, targeting not only government officials and institutions but also ordinary citizens. This revelation led to a diplomatic row between Brazil and the United States, with then-Brazilian President Dilma Rousseff cancelling a state visit to Washington in protest.

In this context, Brazil's backing of the BRICS cable project can be seen as a response to the perceived intrusion on its sovereignty and a desire to reduce dependence on undersea cables controlled by Western countries, which were suspected of being vulnerable to surveillance. By advocating for a cable system under BRICS control, Brazil and its BRICS counterparts aimed to establish a more secure and independent communication infrastructure that would be less susceptible to external surveillance.

While the BRICS cable project ultimately faced challenges and was abandoned, it serves as a notable example of how Brazil sought to assert its interests and protect its citizens' privacy in the face of global surveillance concerns. Brazil's participation in this initiative underscores its willingness to take a leadership role within the BRICS alliance when its national interests and principles of sovereignty are at stake.

CHAPTER 11

The Key to Africa

Despite the early enthusiasm surrounding South Africa's inclusion in the BRIC bloc, which subsequently transformed it into the BRICS in late 2010, the country has faced challenges when assessed through economic metrics. This outcome aligns with Jim O'Neil's earlier predictions, as mentioned in a previous chapter.

South Africa's entry into the BRICS was initially met with optimism and was viewed as a significant step for the African continent. However, over time, it became evident that South Africa's economic performance within the BRICS framework was less robust than that of its fellow member nations. The nation encountered various economic challenges that affected its ability to compete on par with the larger and more rapidly growing economies of Brazil, Russia, India, and China.

Furthermore, South Africa's position as Africa's rising economic giant, a title it once held with pride, has been gradually eclipsed by other emerging economies on the African continent. Nations such as Kenya and Nigeria have made substantial economic strides, overtaking their southern counterpart in terms of economic growth, foreign investment, and regional influence.

This shift in economic dynamics underscores the evolving

landscape of economic power in Africa, where new players are emerging as significant contributors to the continent's growth and development. South Africa's experience within the BRICS alliance reflects the broader economic and geopolitical shifts occurring not only within the group but also on the African continent as a whole.

South Africa's economic struggles within BRICS have raised concerns about the country's vulnerability and dependency on its more economically robust partners, particularly China. The sluggish growth of the South African economy, coupled with internal issues like political corruption and social challenges, has left the nation in a precarious position.

One could argue that this situation benefits certain BRICS members, especially China, which may view a weakened South African government as an opportunity to further its economic and strategic interests in Africa. China's assertive approach on the continent, characterised by extensive investments and infrastructure projects, could exploit South Africa's difficulties, making it a more compliant partner in regional endeavours.

The spectre of neo-colonialism looms large in this context. It's conceivable that South Africa, grappling with its own challenges, may find itself coerced into agreements and partnerships that are heavily skewed in favour of more powerful BRICS members, particularly China and Russia. These nations, driven by their economic and strategic objectives, could use South Africa as a gateway for exerting influence over the African continent, effectively diminishing South Africa's sovereignty.

The reality is that South Africa's political landscape, marked by corruption scandals and governance issues, hasn't provided a strong foundation for independent decision-making and leadership in the BRICS alliance. This lack of agency could exacerbate the nation's reliance on its more influential BRICS counterparts, making it susceptible to their agendas.

In a more pessimistic view, South Africa's once-promising role as Africa's economic powerhouse has been overshadowed by the rise of other nations on the continent, such as Kenya and Nigeria. These emerging economies have overtaken South Africa, further diminishing its regional influence and casting doubt on its ability to represent Africa effectively within BRICS.

The dysfunction within the South African state, particularly in its relations with its BRICS allies, was starkly evident in a notable incident involving Russia. The situation came to a head when South Africa sent mixed messages regarding the execution of an International Criminal Court (ICC) issued warrant against Russian President Vladimir Putin.

The ICC warrant against Putin raised complex legal and diplomatic challenges for South Africa. On one hand, the national courts in South Africa insisted that they would arrest President Putin if he entered the country, as per the ICC warrant. However, the response from the South African government, led by President Cyril Ramaphosa, contradicted this stance.

This contradictory messaging created a diplomatic standoff and added to the perception of dysfunction within the South African state. It left Russia in a difficult position, uncertain about the level of cooperation it could expect from its BRICS partner. The mixed signals not only strained relations between South Africa and Russia but also had wider implications for the BRICS alliance.

This incident highlighted the inherent complexities and contradictions within South Africa's foreign policy and its relations with its BRICS counterparts. It raised questions about the nation's ability to navigate sensitive diplomatic issues while upholding its commitments within the BRICS framework. Ultimately, it served as a sobering reminder of the fragility of international alliances, even among ostensibly like-minded nations.

The complicated relationship between South Africa and its BRICS ally, Russia, was further exacerbated by allegations surrounding the South African government's involvement in supplying weapons for the Russian military invasion of Ukraine. These allegations added another layer of complexity to South Africa's foreign policy and raised concerns about its role in the conflict.

The South African government faced mounting pressure to provide a definitive answer regarding its alleged weapon supplies to Russia. However, the response from South African officials was marked by ambiguity and evasion. This lack of a clear and transparent stance on a matter of international significance deepened suspicions and strained diplomatic relations, not only with Russia but also with other nations in the international community.

The allegations regarding weapon supplies for the Russian invasion of Ukraine put South Africa in a precarious position within the BRICS alliance. It underscored the challenges of balancing its commitment to the alliance with its broader international responsibilities and the need to uphold principles of peace and stability.

Moreover, these allegations further highlighted the issue of corruption within the South African government. The lack of transparency and accountability in such matters eroded trust in the nation's leadership and cast a shadow over its international engagements. Corruption and mismanagement not only hindered South Africa's credibility on the global stage but also had detrimental effects on its domestic governance and stability.

Overall, South Africa's participation in the BRICS alliance has become a delicate balancing act, where economic interests must align with the preservation of democratic norms, sovereignty, and regional influence. The nation's economic struggles, internal challenges, and its complicated relationships with BRICS allies like Russia underscore the vulnerabilities and risks associated with its position in the alliance. South Africa's ability to address these challenges will significantly impact its role within BRICS and its standing as a representative of Africa on the global stage.

Despite the relatively warm relations between South Africa and India within the BRICS alliance, a complex historical legacy exists that dates back to the time when both nations were under British colonial rule. The history of these two countries is intertwined with shared experiences of colonialism and struggles for independence. However, there are also aspects of their shared history that are deeply troubling and continue to affect their relationship.

One of the most significant and troubling aspects of this shared history is the involvement of ethnic Indians in the establishment and enforcement of the apartheid system in South Africa. During the colonial period, many Indians were brought to South Africa as indentured labourers to work on sugar plantations and in other industries. Over time, a significant Indian community developed in South Africa.

However, as South Africa moved toward institutionalising apartheid, which was a system of racial segregation and discrimination, some members of the Indian community became active participants in enforcing these oppressive policies. This collaboration with the apartheid regime has left a lasting scar on the collective memory of South Africa. It stirs painful memories among the masses of the country, particularly among those who suffered under apartheid's oppressive yoke.

The role of some ethnic Indians in supporting apartheid stands in stark contrast to the principles of equality, justice, and anti-colonial resistance that India itself championed during its struggle for independence. India, under the leadership of figures like Mahatma Gandhi, played a pivotal role in the fight against colonialism and racial discrimination. This historical dissonance has, at times, cast a shadow over the relationship between South Africa and India within the BRICS context.

However, it's essential to recognize that the actions of some individuals within the Indian community in South Africa should not be attributed to the entire community or the Indian government. Many Indians in South Africa also actively opposed apartheid and stood in solidarity with the broader anti-apartheid movement.

However, it's crucial to acknowledge that the wounds of history often run deep, and the legacy of collaboration between some ethnic Indians and the apartheid regime continues to cast a long shadow over South Africa's perception of India. While both countries have taken steps to address their respective historical injustices, the scars of the past can still influence their interactions within the BRICS alliance. The spectre of distrust and resentment lingers, reminding us that historical grievances are not easily forgotten or forgiven. These unresolved tensions serve as a sombre backdrop to their participation in BRICS, highlighting the enduring complexities of their relationship despite shared economic goals and global aspirations.

CHAPTER 12

India's Place in the Alliance

India's position within the BRICS alliance has grown increasingly complicated, leading to a sense of pessimism among various quarters. The alliance, once seen as a non-controversial economic partnership, has become a divisive issue among India's policymakers and political pundits, exposing the challenges and dilemmas the nation faces in its international engagements.

For those with more nationalistic leanings, BRICS is viewed as a double-edged sword. While it offers the potential for a united front against perceived Western oppression, it also forces India into alignments and compromises that may not align with its core values and long-term global aspirations. This internal conflict contributes to a sense of disillusionment, as India grapples with the tension between asserting its sovereignty and navigating the complexities of global geopolitics.

On the other hand, politically liberal individuals, too, find themselves disillusioned within the BRICS framework. Some see the alliance as a missed opportunity, where India's voice often gets drowned out in favour of more dominant members like China and Russia. They lament the compromises made to maintain unity within BRICS, which may not always serve

India's best interests.

In this pessimistic view, BRICS has become a challenging tightrope for India to walk. It presents the nation with difficult choices, where economic pragmatism often clashes with its principles and ideals. The internal divisions and external pressures within BRICS have raised doubts about India's ability to pursue its independent global ambitions while participating in this alliance.

In essence, India's involvement in BRICS reflects the broader complexities of its foreign policy, where the pursuit of national interests and the preservation of values often collide, leaving a sense of frustration and uncertainty about the nation's role in the evolving landscape of global geopolitics.

India's hesitance to take on significant leadership roles within alliances like BRICS can be seen as a reflection of a nation that, despite its aspirations on the global stage, remains shackled by the ghosts of past failures. The ill-fated intervention in Sri Lanka serves as a haunting reminder of the perils of military entanglements in the region.

The scars left by the Sri Lankan intervention run deep, not only in terms of the loss of Indian lives and resources but also in the damage it inflicted on India's international reputation. It was a stark lesson in the unforgiving nature of geopolitics, where even the most well-intentioned actions can lead to unintended consequences.

This experience has left India wary of taking on leadership roles that could potentially involve military commitments or long-term interventions within alliances like BRICS. The fear of getting entangled in complex regional conflicts or becoming embroiled in military quagmires has become a spectre that haunts India's foreign policy decisions.

While India's cautious approach aligns with its historical

commitment to non-alignment and strategic autonomy, it also highlights the nation's hesitance to fully embrace its role as a global leader. This reluctance to assume leadership positions, particularly in matters involving military cooperation, has the potential to limit India's influence and impact within international alliances.

In a world where assertiveness often garners respect and influence, India's hesitance to take the lead in military matters may be viewed as a missed opportunity. It leaves India in a position where it may not fully capitalise on its potential to shape the direction of alliances like BRICS or assert its interests on the global stage.

Ultimately, India's caution in matters of military leadership reflects a nation haunted by past failures, hesitant to fully embrace the responsibilities and risks that come with being a global leader. Whether this hesitance serves as a protective shield or a self-imposed limitation on India's rise remains a subject of debate among policymakers and pundits alike.

India's reluctance to take significant leadership roles within the BRICS alliance has inadvertently allowed Russia and China to emerge as de facto leaders, as previously discussed. This passivity on India's part, driven by its longstanding policies of non-interference and reluctance to enter into long-term military alliances, paints a rather bleak picture for the nation's geopolitical influence.

One could speculate that India's caution and hesitation in embracing leadership roles may be influenced by its past misadventures. The ill-fated Indian intervention in Sri Lanka serves as a stark reminder of the risks and consequences associated with military involvement in the affairs of neighbouring countries. This historical baggage has, in many ways, transformed a once-militaristic and interventionist nation into one that treads cautiously on the international stage.

This reticence to assume leadership positions within BRICS has allowed Russia and China, with their more assertive approaches, to seize the reins of the alliance. While India is often hailed as the "world's largest democracy," its failure to assert itself within BRICS has relegated it to a secondary role, overshadowed by the dominant influence of its counterparts.

This lack of initiative and reticence to take on leadership responsibilities is not without consequences. It diminishes India's influence over the alliance's direction and policies, potentially undermining its own national interests. As Russia and China exert greater influence, India risks being sidelined in critical decisions and strategic directions within BRICS.

Furthermore, the dynamics within BRICS, where two major powers with differing geo-political agendas lead the alliance, could create tensions and challenges for India. India's inability to shape the alliance's direction in a way that aligns with its democratic principles and national interests might lead to compromises that do not serve its long-term goals.

In this more pessimistic view, India's passive stance within BRICS not only limits its influence within the alliance but also leaves it vulnerable to the strategic objectives of its dominant partners, particularly Russia and China. It raises questions about India's ability to assert its interests and values on the global stage, despite its size and potential.

India's complex relationship with its fellow BRICS member, China, can be succinctly encapsulated by the saying, "Indians are quick to forget their history and delve into nostalgic fantasies, while the Chinese never forgive or forget." This adage highlights the stark contrast in how the two nations approach their shared historical grievances and memories.

In India's case, there is often a tendency to downplay or even forget historical disputes and conflicts with China. This attitude can be attributed to a desire for improved relations and a focus on future cooperation. Indians may be inclined to move past historical tensions in the hope of building a more amicable and collaborative relationship with their Chinese counterparts. However, this approach can sometimes lead to underestimating the lasting impact of historical events on diplomatic and strategic matters.

On the other hand, China's approach is characterised by a long and unforgiving memory when it comes to historical grievances. The Chinese government and society tend to remember and emphasise past conflicts, territorial disputes, and perceived injustices. This remembrance of history informs China's foreign policy and serves as a source of national identity and pride. China often expects acknowledgment and redressal of perceived historical wrongs from its counterparts as a precondition for stronger relations.

The differing approaches of India and China to their shared history can create significant challenges in their bilateral relations within the BRICS alliance. India's willingness to set aside historical disputes for the sake of cooperation may clash with China's expectation of addressing these issues before progressing. This disconnect can lead to misunderstandings and tensions within the alliance, impacting its ability to act cohesively on various global issues.

In a more realistic view, India's historical amnesia and China's unwavering memory of past conflicts contribute to an underlying tension within BRICS. The failure to reconcile these differing attitudes toward history can hinder the alliance's effectiveness and cohesion, particularly in addressing geopolitical challenges and fostering cooperation among its members. Events like the Opium Wars, which hold great significance in China's historical memory, may be marginalised or overlooked in Indian historical discussions, further exacerbating these tensions.

Furthermore, it's essential to note that China's historical disputes and grievances extend beyond India. The Chinese Communist Party (CCP) has a history of territorial disputes and conflicts with several of its neighbours, including Japan, Taiwan, Vietnam, and the Philippines. These disputes often revolve around territorial claims in the South China Sea, the East China Sea, and border areas.

China's assertive actions in these disputes, such as constructing artificial islands and asserting sovereignty over contested territories, have generated regional tensions and led to concerns among its neighbouring countries. The CCP's unwavering stance on historical grievances, coupled with its assertive posture in territorial disputes, has fueled apprehensions about China's intentions and behaviour in the region.

This broader context of China's disputes with its neighbours adds another layer of complexity to its international relations, including its interactions within the BRICS alliance. India's cautious approach and willingness to downplay historical issues must be seen in the context of China's assertiveness and its historical disputes with multiple countries. These dynamics contribute to the intricate and sometimes precarious nature of India-China relations within the BRICS framework.

In many ways, BRICS has become something of unnecessary baggage that drags India into the actions and policies of both Russia and China, making the "world's largest democracy" appear somewhat hypocritical on the global stage. India often preaches democratic values and human rights to Western nations while concurrently maintaining partnerships and alliances with BRICS partners who may not always align with these principles.

India's stance within BRICS, where it cooperates with Russia and China, both of which have faced international criticism for their handling of democratic norms and human rights, has drawn scrutiny and raised questions about the nation's commitment to its democratic ideals. This dual role can indeed create a perception of hypocrisy in India's foreign policy.

It's worth noting that India has, at times, shown support for leaders and regimes that do not adhere to democratic principles. For example, India's long-standing support for its neighbour Myanmar, despite concerns about the military junta's actions and human rights abuses, has been a subject of international debate. Similarly, India's vocal support for various African dictatorships, often under the banner of "anti-colonialism" or pragmatic engagement, has raised eyebrows among proponents of democracy and human rights.

This complex relationship between India's foreign policy choices, its BRICS alliances, and its commitment to democratic values underscores the intricate web of international politics. Navigating these dynamics can be challenging, especially when the pursuit of national interests and geopolitical considerations intersect with principles of democracy and human rights.

From a pessimistic perspective, India's participation in BRICS may indeed lead to accusations of moral compromise and double standards on the global stage. While India's engagement with BRICS offers economic and strategic advantages, it also places the nation in a position where it must balance its commitment to democratic norms with its partnerships in an alliance that includes countries with differing ideologies and practices.

This balancing act can be a source of criticism and contention, both domestically and internationally, as it forces India to reconcile its role as a champion of democracy with its pragmatic engagements in alliances like BRICS. It serves as a reminder of the complexities and moral dilemmas that often arise in the realm of international diplomacy and foreign policy.

In many ways, India finds itself in a critical and challenging position within the BRICS alliance. The nation faces a dilemma where it must decide whether to take a more assertive leadership role within the alliance, advocating for democratic values and human rights, or continue with its current approach, potentially becoming complicit in its partners' actions that violate these principles.

Taking a more proactive leadership role within BRICS to promote democratic values and human rights would require India to navigate a delicate path. It would involve advocating for changes within the alliance, pushing for more alignment with democratic norms, and using its influence to address concerns about human rights violations among its BRICS partners.

However, such a leadership role could come with its set of challenges and risks. It might strain India's relations with Russia and China, potentially impacting economic and strategic interests. It could also lead to internal debates and divisions within India about the nation's foreign policy priorities and the balance between pragmatism and principle.

On the other hand, maintaining the status quo within BRICS may enable India to preserve its current partnerships and avoid potential conflicts with Russia and China. However, this approach might also mean tolerating actions and policies that run counter to India's professed commitment to democratic values and human rights.

From a more pessimistic perspective, continuing in this manner could raise questions about India's consistency in upholding its democratic principles and might lead to accusations of moral compromise. It could also strain India's relationships with like-minded democracies and impact its standing on the global stage.

In essence, India faces a significant decision within the BRICS alliance – whether to actively push for democratic values and human rights or maintain its current role as a pragmatic partner. This decision will have far-reaching implications for India's foreign policy, its global alliances, and its stance on critical issues of democracy and human rights.

It is important to note that while some populist and nationalistic figures within the Indian elected leadership and bureaucracy may advocate for BRICS as an anti-Western alliance, India has also pursued a separate path when it comes to regional security concerns, particularly in response to Chinese expansion within Asia. One significant development in this regard is the Quadrilateral Security Dialogue (Quad), a strategic security forum that includes Australia, India, Japan, and the United States. The Quad was initially formed in 2007 as a means to address shared security challenges in the Indo-Pacific region and to contain Chinese influence.

However, the Quad's history has been marked by periods of instability. After its initial formation, the dialogue partnership dissolved in 2008 due to concerns and reservations among member countries. It was subsequently reinstated in 2017 as geopolitical dynamics evolved and concerns about Chinese expansion in the region grew more pronounced.

The Quad's objectives include promoting a free and open Indo-Pacific, ensuring maritime security, and enhancing regional stability. While the Quad primarily focuses on security and defence cooperation, it also engages in discussions related to economic development and infrastructure projects in the Indo-Pacific region.

India's participation in the Quad demonstrates its willingness to collaborate with like-minded nations, including the United States and Japan, to address regional security challenges and counterbalance Chinese expansion in the Asian sphere of influence. This stance reflects India's strategic interests and its commitment to upholding a rules-based international order in the Indo-Pacific. However, it is worth noting that India's engagement in the Quad is just one aspect of its broader foreign policy approach, and the stability of this partnership may continue to evolve in response to changing geopolitical dynamics.

CHAPTER 13

United in Corruption

It is no secret that despite all their posturing towards anti-corruption and international transparency, the BRICS members are well known for their high levels of corruption, with them regularly ranking considerably lower than their western counterparts according to the Corruption Perceptions Index. In a somewhat macabre sense, this is one of the few unifying factors among these five member countries. This pervasive issue of corruption has far-reaching implications, both domestically and internationally, for each of the BRICS nations.

Domestically, corruption erodes public trust in government institutions, hinders economic development, and perpetuates social inequalities. It diverts resources away from essential public services, such as healthcare and education, and undermines the rule of law. In many BRICS countries, corruption scandals have shaken political stability and fueled public protests, highlighting the pressing need for meaningful anti-corruption reforms.

In many BRICS countries, corruption scandals have not only shaken political stability but have also fueled widespread public protests. Citizens, frustrated by the blatant abuse of power and resources, take to the streets to demand accountability and transparency. These protests underscore the pressing need for meaningful anti-corruption reforms that address both the symptoms and root causes of corruption.

On the international stage, the prevalence of corruption within BRICS member nations raises concerns about their adherence to global norms and standards. It can hinder international cooperation and diplomatic efforts, especially when corruption allegations involve cross-border transactions or bribery of foreign officials. Additionally, it can tarnish the reputation of the BRICS alliance as a whole, as it calls into question the commitment of member nations to ethical governance and transparency.

It could be argued that the eventual halt of the promising growth initially exhibited by Brazil, Russia, India, and China is somewhat ironic, given that Jim O'Neill's initial report played a significant role in the eventual formal creation of the BRICS alliance. O'Neill's report identified these four nations as emerging economic powerhouses, with expectations of sustained growth and increasing global influence.

Brazil's economic performance within the BRICS alliance has been marked by periods of economic slowdowns and political turbulence. High inflation rates, persistent fiscal deficits, and corruption scandals have been among the key factors contributing to Brazil's economic woes. These domestic challenges not only hindered economic growth but also eroded investor confidence in the country.

One of the most notable economic challenges facing Brazil was its struggle with high inflation. Double-digit inflation rates persisted for years, eroding the purchasing power of citizens and creating uncertainty in the business environment. Efforts to curb inflation often involved tight monetary policies that constrained economic growth and investment.

Fiscal deficits also posed a significant challenge. Brazil grappled with budget shortfalls, making it difficult to fund essential public services and infrastructure projects. The government faced tough decisions regarding budget allocations and austerity measures, which often fueled public discontent and protests.

Corruption scandals further exacerbated Brazil's economic and political woes. High-profile investigations, such as the Operation Car Wash probe, uncovered widespread corruption involving top politicians and business leaders. These scandals not only eroded public trust in institutions but also led to political instability and uncertainty.

In this context, Brazil's ability to play a leading role within the BRICS alliance was hampered. The nation turned its focus inward to address pressing economic and political challenges, diverting attention and resources away from international initiatives. As a result, Brazil's influence within the BRICS grouping was diminished during these tumultuous periods.

While Brazil has made efforts to address some of these economic and governance issues, such as implementing anti-corruption measures and pursuing economic reforms, the road to recovery has been uneven. Economic and political stability remains a work in progress, and Brazil's role within BRICS continues to be influenced by its domestic challenges and the need for sustained reforms.

Russia, another prominent member of the BRICS alliance, confronted a distinctive set of challenges that significantly influenced its role within the group. The annexation of Crimea in 2014 and Russia's involvement in the conflict in Eastern Ukraine were pivotal events that reshaped its international standing and relationships with Western nations.

The annexation of Crimea, in particular, triggered a swift

and robust international response. Western nations, including the United States and European Union, imposed economic sanctions on Russia in protest of its actions. These sanctions targeted key sectors of the Russian economy and individuals closely associated with the Kremlin. The sanctions regime not only had economic repercussions but also generated geopolitical tensions and diplomatic frictions between Russia and Western powers.

These developments raised fundamental questions about Russia's position and behaviour within the BRICS framework. While the BRICS alliance was established to promote cooperation among emerging economies, Russia's actions in Crimea and Ukraine put it at odds with the principles of international law and territorial integrity that the alliance ostensibly supported.

The annexation of Crimea and the ongoing conflict in Eastern Ukraine cast a shadow over the BRICS grouping's commitment to these principles, creating a significant dilemma for the member nations. Russia's actions generated concerns about the alliance's ability to maintain a unified stance on critical issues, particularly those involving geopolitical conflicts and territorial disputes.

Within the BRICS context, the Ukraine crisis prompted discussions and debates about how member nations should address the situation. While some BRICS members adopted a cautious and neutral stance, others expressed concerns about Russia's actions and emphasised the importance of respecting international norms. These differing viewpoints underscored the complexities of maintaining cohesion within the alliance when confronted with divisive geopolitical issues.

For Russia, the Ukraine crisis highlighted the challenges of balancing its strategic interests with its role within BRICS. While the alliance offered opportunities for economic cooperation and a platform for engagement with other emerging powers, it also exposed Russia to scrutiny and diplomatic pressures related to its foreign policy choices.

India, on the other hand, experienced phases of rapid economic growth, positioning itself as one of the world's fastest-growing major economies. The country's demographic dividend, characterised by a young and growing population, alongside the burgeoning middle class and advancements in technology, fueled optimism about its long-term economic prospects. India's economic liberalisation and pro-business reforms, initiated in the early 1990s, attracted foreign investment, spurred entrepreneurship, and fostered a dynamic business environment.

However, India's growth story was not without its share of challenges and complexities. Income inequality remained a persistent and pressing issue, with substantial disparities between the urban and rural populations. While the urban centres experienced rapid economic growth and increased prosperity, rural areas faced challenges related to limited access to quality education, healthcare, and basic infrastructure.

Bureaucratic hurdles and complex regulations often hindered the ease of doing business in India. Navigating administrative processes and obtaining necessary approvals could be time-consuming and unpredictable, deterring both domestic and foreign investors. Additionally, the country's legal and regulatory environment occasionally posed challenges, requiring businesses to navigate a complex web of laws and compliance requirements.

Infrastructure development, although gradually improving, lagged behind the demands of a rapidly growing economy. Inadequate transportation networks, insufficient energy supply, and other infrastructure bottlenecks constrained economic growth and posed logistical challenges for businesses.

Addressing these infrastructure deficiencies remained a priority for policymakers, but progress was often hampered by financial constraints and bureaucratic delays.

Political and administrative obstacles, at times, led to delays in critical projects and policy implementations. India's federal structure of governance, with powers divided between the central and state governments, occasionally resulted in coordination challenges and variations in policy implementation across different regions.

China, often heralded as the economic powerhouse of the BRICS, embarked on a remarkable economic expansion that lifted millions out of poverty and dramatically transformed its global standing. The nation's rapid industrialization, export-led growth, and massive infrastructure projects contributed to its emergence as the world's second-largest economy, only trailing behind the United States. China's economic ascent served as a source of inspiration for other BRICS member nations, demonstrating the potential for emerging economies to significantly influence and reshape the global economic landscape.

However, amid its impressive growth, concerns began to surface about the sustainability of China's economic model. The country's heavy reliance on exports and the expansion of resource-intensive industries raised alarming questions about environmental sustainability, resource depletion, and overcapacity. As China became a major global player in manufacturing and trade, issues related to the quality of its exports, including product safety and intellectual property rights, garnered international attention.

Mounting debt levels, especially within the corporate sector, became a growing source of concern. The rapid accumulation of debt raised worries about financial stability and the potential for a debt crisis that could reverberate through the global economy.

Simultaneously, income inequality within China continued to widen, with significant disparities between urban and rural areas, sparking social and political challenges that required careful management.

The evolving geopolitical dynamics in the Asia-Pacific region and China's assertive foreign policy, particularly in territorial disputes in the South China Sea, added another layer of complexity to the BRICS alliance. While China's economic prowess was undeniable, questions arose about how its geopolitical ambitions aligned with the interests of other BRICS members and the broader international community.

South Africa, by far, ranks as the worst performer among the BRICS nations, both in economic and social terms. While the BRICS alliance was initially formed with the objective of fostering cooperation among emerging economies, South Africa's performance across various key indicators has consistently lagged behind that of its fellow member nations.

Economically, South Africa has grappled with challenges that have hindered its ability to match the robust growth rates seen in countries like China and India. High levels of unemployment, income inequality, and a volatile currency have presented significant obstacles to sustained economic progress. The nation has faced difficulties in attracting foreign investment and addressing deep-seated structural issues that continue to impede its economic development.

Furthermore, on the social front, South Africa confronts a range of pressing challenges, including issues related to poverty, healthcare, education, and crime. The enduring legacy of apartheid and historical inequalities continue to exert influence on social dynamics within the country. While there have been notable strides in some areas, significant disparities persist, and the pursuit of social development remains a complex and ongoing endeavour.

These developments raise questions about the long-term prospects of the BRICS alliance and the ability of its member nations to maintain their economic momentum. While the BRICS grouping continues to serve as a platform for cooperation and dialogue, it also highlights the complexities and uncertainties of the global economic landscape.

The initial optimism that surrounded the BRICS concept, driven by expectations of unceasing growth and influence, has been tempered by the realities of economic and geopolitical challenges. The future of the BRICS alliance will depend on the ability of its member nations to adapt to changing circumstances and work together to address common issues while navigating their individual economic and political trajectories.

CHAPTER 14

A Common Currency?

The notion of a common currency among BRICS member nations has been a recurring topic of discussion, often accompanied by a degree of enthusiasm and expectation. However, the practical challenges of establishing such a unified monetary policy project are considerable, and the dominance of the U.S. dollar in the global financial system presents a significant barrier to any potential alternative currency.

While some might perceive the discussion of a BRICS reserve currency as a relatively recent development, it is essential to note that this idea was among the early discussions within the BRIC grouping itself, even before it expanded to include South Africa. Despite initial conversations and proposals, no BRICS currency was launched during the first official meeting of the BRICS nations in 2009.

These early considerations regarding a common currency within BRICS may have been influenced or inspired by the introduction of the Euro as a common currency in the European Union (EU) at the end of the 20th century. It's possible that the BRIC and later BRICS nations saw themselves as a "more inclusive" version of regional economic cooperation, similar in some respects to the EU.

This chapter explores the various plans and proposals put forth by BRICS member nations regarding a common currency and delves into the significant challenges they face in realising such an endeavour. The ongoing dominance of the U.S. dollar in global trade and finance, along with the economic complexities within each BRICS nation, make the path to a unified currency a complex and formidable one.

Despite some analysts portraying BRICS as a rising power that challenges the dominance of Western nations, it's essential to recognize the economic challenges faced by individual BRICS member states. These challenges include economic issues, political tensions, and varying degrees of cooperation among the member nations themselves. The portrayal of BRICS as a unified and unassailable force oversimplifies a more nuanced and multifaceted reality.

One of the proposals considered for a common BRICS currency is a gold-backed currency. This concept bears similarities to the historical gold standard, where the value of a nation's currency is directly tied to a specific quantity of gold held in reserves. In this case, the idea is that the BRICS member nations would jointly introduce a new currency that is pegged to the price of gold and backed by the combined national gold reserves of each member.

While this proposal may seem appealing in theory, it carries several disadvantages and challenges, reminiscent of the issues associated with the traditional gold standard:

- Limited Flexibility: A gold-backed currency restricts a nation's ability to adjust its money supply to respond to changing economic conditions. It ties the currency's value to the quantity of gold, which may not align with the economic needs of a nation.

- Vulnerability to Supply Constraints: The value of a gold-backed currency can be influenced by fluctuations in the global gold supply. Changes in gold production or mining activities can impact the currency's stability.

- Economic Constraints: Under a gold standard, countries often had to maintain large gold reserves to back their currency, which could limit their ability to invest in other areas, such as infrastructure or social programs.

- Deflationary Pressures: A gold-backed currency can lead to deflationary pressures, as the money supply is limited by the availability of gold. Deflation can hinder economic growth and job creation.

- Inflexible Exchange Rates: Fixed exchange rates tied to gold can lead to balance of payments issues, as countries may struggle to adjust their exchange rates to address trade imbalances.

- Vulnerability to Speculation: Speculative trading in gold markets can lead to rapid fluctuations in the currency's value, creating instability in the broader economy.

- Limited Monetary Policy Tools: Central banks have fewer tools to influence economic conditions when their currency is tied to a gold standard. This limitation can hinder their ability to respond to economic crises.

Given these drawbacks, the adoption of a gold-backed currency within the BRICS alliance would present significant challenges and could have adverse effects on the economic policies and flexibility of member nations. While the idea of a gold-backed currency may hold theoretical appeal, the practical implications and limitations make it a less viable option in today's complex global economic landscape.

The uneven distribution of gold reserves among BRICS member

nations in the context of a hypothetical gold-backed currency raises significant concerns and potential challenges that could severely impact the viability of such a currency system.

One of the most pressing issues is the likelihood of larger BRICS players, such as China and Russia, leveraging their substantial gold reserves to exert dominance over the currency's policies and value. This scenario could lead to a stark power imbalance within the BRICS alliance, with smaller nations like South Africa finding themselves at a severe disadvantage. Smaller members may have limited control and influence over the currency, essentially becoming subservient to the economic interests and decisions of their more prominent counterparts.

Furthermore, this unequal distribution of gold reserves threatens to deepen existing economic disparities among BRICS nations. Rather than fostering cooperation and economic growth, the gold-backed currency system could exacerbate these inequalities. The economic power dynamic within BRICS could become increasingly skewed, potentially resulting in conflicts and tensions among member states.

In such a scenario, the BRICS alliance may struggle to maintain its cohesion and relevance on the global stage. Smaller nations may grow increasingly resentful and marginalised, while larger members assert their dominance. This could lead to disagreements, infighting, and a lack of consensus on key economic and financial issues, ultimately undermining the very foundation of the BRICS alliance.

Moreover, the unequal distribution of gold reserves could deter other emerging economies from considering membership in BRICS, viewing it as an exclusive club where a few major players dictate the rules. This lack of inclusivity could limit the alliance's ability to expand and diversify its membership, further isolating it on the global economic landscape.

The notion that a gold-backed currency could replace the US

dollar as the world's primary reserve currency is indeed a challenging proposition, if not a far-fetched fantasy. Several critical factors make it highly improbable and virtually unachievable in the foreseeable future.

One of the primary obstacles is the existing global financial infrastructure, where gold is primarily traded and valued in US dollars. This longstanding tradition and practice have created a deep interdependence between gold markets and the US currency. Any attempt by BRICS or any other alliance to introduce a gold-backed currency would inevitably face the challenge of breaking this entrenched linkage.

In essence, a gold-backed BRICS currency would find itself at the mercy of the very system it aims to replace. The global reliance on the US dollar as the world's primary reserve currency has been firmly established for decades, with most international transactions, trade agreements, and financial instruments denominated in dollars. Attempting to introduce a new gold-backed currency would require dismantling this extensive infrastructure, a task that would encounter substantial resistance and complexity.

Moreover, the US dollar's status as the world's reserve currency is supported not only by tradition and convenience but also by the economic and political stability of the United States. Investors and central banks around the world have historically viewed the US dollar as a safe and reliable store of value. This perception is grounded in the strength of the US economy, the stability of its political institutions, and the depth of its financial markets. Replacing the dollar with a new currency, even if backed by gold, would necessitate building a comparable level of confidence and trust, a process that could take decades, if not longer.

Additionally, the transition to a gold-backed currency would introduce new challenges related to the management of gold reserves, exchange rates, and monetary policy coordination among BRICS member nations. These complexities would require a high degree of cooperation and alignment, which, as discussed earlier, could be hampered by power imbalances and economic disparities within the alliance.

In summary, while the idea of a gold-backed currency replacing the US dollar may capture the imagination of some, the practical realities and complexities of such a transition make it a highly implausible scenario. The entrenched position of the US dollar in the global financial system, along with the economic and political challenges involved, render this concept more of a fantasy than a feasible alternative in the foreseeable future.

Rumours about a potential BRICS-backed cryptocurrency have indeed circulated in recent years, often fueled by the hype surrounding cryptocurrencies and blockchain technology. However, it's important to approach such rumours with a critical perspective, as the actual implementation of a BRICS-backed cryptocurrency faces numerous challenges and complexities.

Cryptocurrencies, such as Bitcoin and Ethereum, have gained attention for their potential to revolutionise the financial industry and enable more efficient cross-border transactions. Some proponents have suggested that a BRICS cryptocurrency could offer advantages such as reduced dependence on traditional banking systems, enhanced security, and increased financial inclusivity.

Despite these potential benefits, several significant hurdles would need to be overcome for a BRICS-backed cryptocurrency to become a reality. These challenges include:

Regulatory and Legal Frameworks: Each BRICS member nation has its regulatory and legal framework for cryptocurrencies, which varies significantly. Harmonising these diverse regulatory environments would be a complex and time-consuming process.

- Technological Infrastructure: Developing and maintaining the technological infrastructure for a BRICS cryptocurrency, including blockchain technology and secure networks, would require substantial investments and expertise.

- Monetary Policy Coordination: BRICS member nations have distinct monetary policies and economic objectives. Coordinating these policies to support a common cryptocurrency would be challenging, especially given varying economic conditions.

- Security Concerns: Ensuring the security of a BRICS cryptocurrency would be paramount, as cryptocurrencies are vulnerable to hacking and cyberattacks. Robust security measures and protocols would be necessary to protect the currency's integrity.

- International Acceptance: Achieving global acceptance of a BRICS cryptocurrency would be difficult, as it would need to compete with established cryptocurrencies like Bitcoin and traditional fiat currencies. Building trust and adoption among international businesses, financial institutions, and consumers would take time.

- Public Perception: Cryptocurrencies often face scepticism and uncertainty among the general public due to their association with price volatility and illegal activities. Addressing these concerns and fostering public trust would be crucial.

While discussions about a BRICS-backed cryptocurrency may have generated attention, it's essential to recognize that the practical implementation of such a plan would be a complex and long-term endeavour. As of the writing of this book, no official announcement or concrete steps had been taken by BRICS member nations to create a unified cryptocurrency. Therefore, any rumours or discussions should be viewed with caution until there is clear and official information on the matter.

A more realistic possibility for a unified BRICS currency could involve the establishment of a traditional currency backed by the New Development Bank, which would act as a central bank for this economic bloc. In theory, this arrangement might resemble the European Union and the Euro. However, while it may seem workable on paper, it gives rise to more problems than it resolves.

The primary issue is that such a system could potentially put the other BRICS nations at the mercy of China. Unlike the European Union, where member nations share historical ties, common values, and often similar political systems, the BRICS members have significant differences. These differences encompass political ideologies, economic structures, and strategic interests.

China's economic and political dominance within the BRICS alliance, particularly in comparison to the other member nations, could create an uneven power dynamic. This could result in a scenario where China wields disproportionate influence over the proposed unified currency and the economic policies of the BRICS bloc.

Additionally, the lack of a shared history of cooperation and mutual trust among BRICS member nations could hinder their ability to effectively govern and manage a common currency. Unlike the European Union, where decades of integration and collaboration have occurred, the BRICS nations have not yet developed a similar level of institutional cohesion, and in certain cases could be considered regional rivals.

Moreover, concerns about issues such as economic competition, trade imbalances, and potential currency manipulation could further complicate the functioning of a unified BRICS currency backed by the New Development Bank.

While the idea of a common currency might hold appeal as a symbol of economic unity, the practical challenges and the risk of imbalances in influence among member nations make it a complex and potentially contentious proposition. It would require careful negotiation, coordination, and trust-building among the BRICS nations, factors that might not align with their current geopolitical dynamics and differing national priorities.

It's also plausible that the concept of a BRICS currency is somewhat exaggerated, and in practice, it might represent more of a joint-national reserve currency used to facilitate trade between BRICS member nations. The rhetoric surrounding this hypothetical currency replacing the US dollar could be, to a large extent, a populist talking point employed by nationalistic politicians to energise their supporters.

Furthermore, the desire for a diminishing US-led western hegemony is shared by many adversaries of the United States. This aspiration can lead to the illusion that a BRICS currency could supplant the US dollar (or other major Western currencies like the Euro or Pound Sterling), a scenario that they fervently hope would become a reality. In reality, challenging the supremacy of these established global reserve currencies is an incredibly complex undertaking, with numerous economic, financial, and geopolitical obstacles to overcome.

The global financial system is deeply entrenched with the US dollar as the primary reserve currency, and altering this status quo would require not only substantial economic and monetary reforms but also a broad international consensus. The strength and stability of the US economy, the size and liquidity of US financial markets, and the widespread use of the dollar in international trade all contribute to its dominance.

While discussions about a BRICS currency may continue as a symbolic expression of economic cooperation among these emerging economies, the practical challenges of challenging the dollar's hegemony remain formidable. It's essential to separate aspirational rhetoric from the complex realities of global finance and the established international monetary order.

CHAPTER 15

BRICS+

The expansion of the BRICS alliance, often referred to as BRICS+, represents a significant development in the realm of international geopolitics and economics. While the BRICS grouping initially brought together some of the world's largest emerging markets, its leadership has taken steps to incorporate new members, expanding its influence and reach.

The inclusion of new members in BRICS+ is noteworthy not only for its numerical expansion but also for the diversity of applicant nations in terms of political ideologies and economic strength. These new entrants are poised to join the BRICS alliance in the early months of 2024, reshaping the dynamics of this economic bloc.

This chapter aims to delve into the profiles of the six "new" members who are set to join BRICS+, providing insights into their political orientations, economic standing, and potential implications for the existing BRICS nations. The addition of these new members introduces fresh perspectives, challenges, and opportunities for the BRICS+ alliance, making it a crucial development to watch in the evolving landscape of global economics and diplomacy.

The inclusion of Argentina, Egypt, Ethiopia, Iran, Saudi Arabia, and the United Arab Emirates as new members of BRICS+ presents a complex and potentially challenging dynamic. These nations, each with its own set of unique characteristics, political ideologies, and economic strengths, bring a level of diversity that may prove to be a double-edged sword.

While the expansion of BRICS+ may be viewed as a symbol of evolving international cooperation, it also raises questions about the feasibility of effective collaboration among such dissimilar countries. The potential for conflicting interests, competing regional influences, and differing priorities looms large, casting a shadow of uncertainty over the unity and effectiveness of this expanded alliance.

As we delve into the profiles of these new BRICS+ members in the chapters that follow, it becomes apparent that their inclusion may introduce complexities that challenge the cohesion of the alliance. The divergent paths and ambitions of these nations could give rise to tensions and disagreements within BRICS+, potentially hindering its ability to achieve its objectives.

While the global stage watches with interest, it remains to be seen whether this expanded alliance will successfully navigate the hurdles posed by its newfound diversity or if it will ultimately succumb to the weight of its disparate members' ambitions and interests.

Until early 2020, the BRICS bloc displayed a marked reluctance and lacked established protocols for the inclusion of new members into its existing structure. There was no formal application process in place for BRICS membership. Instead, any government aspiring to join this alliance faced the formidable hurdle of securing unanimous approval from all existing BRICS members—Brazil, Russia, India, China, and South Africa—in order to receive an invitation.

This exclusive approach, where each member held veto power over potential new entrants, underscored the cautious and selective nature of BRICS expansion. It reflected the recognition that any additions to the alliance could carry profound implications for its dynamics, objectives, and the cohesion of its member states. Consequently, the path to BRICS membership was not just daunting but also contingent on the unanimous consent of the existing participants, ensuring that only those nations with the unanimous support of all BRICS members could even contemplate joining this exclusive club.

Argentina:

Argentina's economic woes have been exacerbated by a history of defaulting on its sovereign debt, including a high-profile default in 2001, one of the largest in global financial history. These debt crises have made it challenging for Argentina to access international capital markets on favourable terms, limiting its ability to fund essential public services and infrastructure development. While the country has recently reached debt restructuring agreements with creditors, its history of defaults continues to affect investor confidence and its overall economic stability.

Moreover, Argentina's internal political landscape has been characterised by polarisation and frequent changes in leadership and policy direction. This political instability has made it difficult to implement long-term economic reforms and maintain consistency in economic policies, which are crucial for attracting foreign investment and fostering economic growth.

The country's economic challenges have also led to social unrest and public protests, as citizens grapple with the impact of inflation, currency devaluation, and unemployment. Addressing these social and economic issues requires significant government attention and resources, raising questions about Argentina's capacity to actively engage and contribute to the

BRICS alliance's objectives.

In light of these complexities, the inclusion of Argentina in the BRICS+ framework warrants careful consideration. While Argentina brings economic heft and regional influence to the table, its internal challenges and uncertainties may present hurdles to its full integration into the alliance. BRICS members will need to assess how Argentina's participation aligns with the group's objectives and whether the benefits of its inclusion outweigh the potential risks and disruptions it may introduce. The dynamics of this evolving alliance will continue to shape the future role of Argentina within BRICS and its ability to contribute to the collective goals of the group.

Argentina's dire economic state, characterised by rising hyperinflation, a thriving black market for US dollars, widespread national unrest, and economic uncertainty, presents significant challenges for its potential inclusion in the BRICS alliance. As the second-largest South American economy, Argentina's economic stability is crucial for the overall cohesion and effectiveness of the BRICS grouping.

Additionally, the opposition expressed by two prominent presidential candidates in Argentina raises doubts about the country's commitment to joining BRICS and aligning with the alliance's objectives. This internal division underscores the potential political obstacles that Argentina may face in becoming a reliable member of the BRICS community.

Furthermore, Argentina's history of financial crises and defaults on sovereign debt has eroded confidence in its financial stability, impacting its ability to attract foreign investment and contribute positively to BRICS initiatives. The country's economic challenges, coupled with its internal political dynamics, may introduce instability into the alliance, potentially undermining its collective goals.

In conclusion, while Argentina's economic and regional

influence could be seen as an asset to BRICS, its current economic woes and internal political divisions raise valid concerns about the feasibility and stability of its inclusion in the alliance. BRICS members will need to carefully evaluate the potential risks and benefits of Argentina's participation and consider whether the country can effectively contribute to the group's objectives while addressing its pressing domestic issues.

Egypt:

Egypt's decision to seek full membership in the BRICS alliance, building upon its existing role as a minority stakeholder in the New Development Bank (NDB), highlights its natural progression within the group. Egypt's established positive relations with the existing BRICS members have paved the way for its inclusion as a full member. However, it's essential to recognize that Egypt's position within BRICS, while promising, presents potential challenges and complexities.

One of the primary considerations is Egypt's internal stability and political dynamics. The country has experienced periods of political unrest and leadership transitions in recent years, raising questions about its long-term political stability. Ensuring Egypt can provide stable and consistent governance is vital for its effective participation in international alliances like BRICS.

Moreover, Egypt's economic performance and development challenges warrant careful assessment. While the country has made progress in various areas, it still faces economic disparities, high youth unemployment, and significant infrastructure needs. BRICS members should evaluate how Egypt's full membership aligns with the group's economic objectives and assess its potential contributions to the alliance's development initiatives.

Additionally, Egypt's geopolitical positioning in the Middle East introduces additional complexities into the BRICS alliance. The region has been characterised by conflicts and rivalries, and Egypt's role in regional politics could impact BRICS dynamics, particularly concerning its relationships with other BRICS members like Russia and China.

While Egypt's inclusion offers benefits, such as its strategic location, access to the Suez Canal, and historical ties to Africa and the Middle East, these factors require thorough consideration. They could create new opportunities for BRICS in terms of trade, investment, and regional influence but may also introduce geopolitical challenges.

In summary, Egypt's decision to pursue full membership in BRICS, building upon its existing role, reflects a significant development. BRICS members should carefully evaluate Egypt's political stability, economic capacity, and regional positioning, as the country's participation aligns with the group's objectives and enhances its collective strength in the global arena.

Ethiopia:

Ethiopia's path to becoming an official member of the BRICS alliance in 2024 presents a complex and challenging situation that could have more detrimental consequences than initially anticipated. While Ethiopia was once considered a stabilising force in a conflict-prone region of Africa, its recent developments have raised alarm bells regarding its stability and the potential implications of its inclusion in BRICS.

Ethiopia finds itself embroiled in internal strife characterised by systematic ethnic violence, economic crises, and military conflicts with neighbouring nations. The ongoing conflict in the Tigray region and other parts of the country has drawn international condemnation and calls for urgent humanitarian intervention. Ethiopia's internal instability appears to be worsening, and there are growing doubts about its commitment and ability to address these complex and deeply rooted issues.

The inclusion of Ethiopia in BRICS could prove to be a significant liability for the existing five members. BRICS nations often collaborate on matters of global importance, including issues related to peace, security, and human rights. Ethiopia's internal challenges, particularly those involving ethnic minorities and conflict, could potentially make BRICS members complicit in or responsible for addressing severe human rights violations and conflicts within Ethiopia. This could strain the alliance's relationships and credibility on the international stage.

Furthermore, Ethiopia's strategic location in the Horn of Africa introduces a complex geopolitical dimension to the BRICS alliance. While it may offer opportunities for increased trade, investment, and regional influence, it also brings about geopolitical complexities, particularly concerning the country's relations with other African nations and global powers. The BRICS alliance might find itself entangled in regional disputes and rivalries that could divert its focus from its core objectives.

BRICS members now face a dilemma in evaluating Ethiopia's role within the alliance. They must weigh the potential benefits against the severe liabilities of Ethiopia's membership. Addressing Ethiopia's internal challenges and conflicts will likely require a significant diplomatic and humanitarian effort, potentially diverting resources and attention away from other global issues.

In summary, Ethiopia's inclusion in BRICS, while initially seen as an opportunity, now appears to carry significant risks and challenges that could strain the alliance's unity and credibility. As Ethiopia's internal situation deteriorates, BRICS members must grapple with the harsh reality that their decision to welcome Ethiopia into the fold may have far-reaching and detrimental consequences.

Iran and Saudi Arabia

The 2023 deal brokered by Chinese leadership between Saudi Arabia and Iran, aimed at reducing tensions between these two Middle Eastern rivals, appears to be more about public relations than substantial peace. This agreement builds upon earlier bilateral deals signed in 1998 and 2001, suggesting that underlying tensions persist despite diplomatic efforts.

It's crucial to recognize that Saudi Arabia and Iran are embroiled in a regional cold war that spans the Middle East. Both nations have engaged in proxy conflicts and direct interventions, committing numerous war crimes in their pursuit of geopolitical dominance. These hostilities stretch from Syria to Yemen, resulting in widespread suffering and instability.

While the rivalry between Saudi Arabia and Iran has geopolitical objectives, it is rooted in religious differences. Saudi Arabia is a monarchy governed with the support of fundamentalist Wahhabi clerics, while Iran is an extremist Shia Islamic theocracy that operates under the facade of democracy. Both nations have concerning records on human rights, with societal development and individual freedoms often falling short of modern standards.

Incorporating Saudi Arabia and Iran into BRICS may offer economic advantages, including access to Middle Eastern natural resources and crude oil reserves. However, this move could introduce more problems than it solves. The primary concern is that the longstanding rivalry between these two nations would create division within the BRICS alliance. Additionally, BRICS could be seen as complicit in the human rights violations perpetrated by Saudi Arabia and Iran, undermining the alliance's credibility.

Iran's potential inclusion presents a unique challenge, as it is considered a pariah state in the international community. Iran's hostile rhetoric toward the West and support for extremist groups designated as terrorist organisations further complicate its integration into an economic alliance like BRICS.

In summary, while bringing Saudi Arabia and Iran into BRICS might offer economic benefits, the deep-rooted regional rivalry, human rights concerns, and the potential for divisive influences within the alliance could pose significant challenges. BRICS would need to carefully consider the consequences of including these Middle Eastern powers and how it might impact its objectives and reputation on the global stage. The inclusion of Saudi Arabia and Iran could introduce complexities that overshadow any economic advantages, potentially hampering the alliance's unity and effectiveness.

The United Arab Emirates:

The United Arab Emirates (UAE) may have perceived its potential inclusion in the BRICS economic bloc as an opportunity to diversify its economy away from heavy reliance on petroleum. Moreover, UAE's leadership could have viewed joining BRICS as a strategic move to attract more investments for their numerous infrastructure and real estate projects, particularly from affluent members of the established BRICS nations. Speculatively, the UAE's leadership might have also seen citizens of BRICS member nations as potential tourists who could contribute to the growth of their tourism industry.

Notably, similar to Egypt, the United Arab Emirates already holds a minority stake in the New Development Bank. Thus, becoming a full BRICS member in 2024 seems like a natural progression.

However, it's important to highlight that, akin to its northern neighbour and GCC partner, Saudi Arabia, the United Arab Emirates operates as an absolute monarchy and faces criticisms regarding its human rights record. Reports have emerged of government critics being detained and subjected to torture, families experiencing harassment by state security apparatuses, and instances of forced disappearances. Fundamental individual rights, such as freedom of assembly, association, the press, expression, and religion, face severe restrictions in the UAE.

This context raises questions about how the inclusion of the United Arab Emirates into the BRICS alliance aligns with the bloc's principles and goals. While economic diversification and investment opportunities may be attractive aspects, concerns related to human rights and individual freedoms within the UAE could potentially conflict with the values and norms upheld by the BRICS alliance. The impact of such dynamics on the alliance's cohesion and ability to pursue its objectives warrants careful consideration by all member nations.

The unanimous invitation of all six new members into the expanded BRICS alliance does raise a moral dilemma and prompts questions about the motives and considerations of the original BRICS nations. It appears that the expansion has been driven, at least in part, by short-term economic and strategic interests, such as access to resources and markets, investment opportunities, and geopolitical influence. However, these expansions have occurred without clear mechanisms for addressing ethical concerns and ensuring long-term geopolitical stability.

The inclusion of nations with diverse political systems, human rights records, and regional interests, such as Saudi Arabia and Iran, presents challenges to the unity and coherence of the alliance. It raises questions about whether the BRICS alliance will prioritise economic and strategic interests over ethical considerations and whether it can effectively address the potential conflicts and divergent values among its members.

Moreover, the rapid expansion of the alliance without adequate deliberation on ethical concerns and long-term stability could risk diluting the original vision and objectives of BRICS. It may lead to a situation where the alliance becomes less focused on promoting shared values and more driven by individual members' self-interests.

Ultimately, the BRICS alliance faces a delicate balancing act between pursuing economic and strategic benefits through expansion and upholding its principles and ethical standards. The success and sustainability of this expanded alliance will depend on how effectively it navigates these complex dynamics and ensures that ethical concerns and long-term stability are not sacrificed for short-term gains.

CHAPTER 16

The One That Got Away

Indonesia's rejection of an invitation to join the BRICS economic bloc carries significant and potentially troubling implications for the alliance's expansion and influence, particularly in Southeast Asia. This strategic move by the Indonesian leadership highlights their perception of BRICS as an anti-Western bloc, which is underscored by the alliance's vocal stance on de-dollarization and the inclusion of members like Russia and China—nations that have often clashed with Western values and the notion of sovereignty.

This development serves as a stark reminder of the deepening divide within the BRICS alliance. While BRICS was initially conceived as an economic bloc, its members' geopolitical orientations and values have become increasingly divergent, posing a challenge to the alliance's unity. Some members, including several of the original five, are actively seeking to distance themselves from the Western sphere of influence, even if it means compromising on established democratic norms, human rights, and other basic freedoms.

Indonesia's refusal to join BRICS is a clear indication that the alliance's principles and priorities are at odds with those of certain emerging economic powers. It highlights the intricate dynamics at play within this expanding alliance and raises concerns about a concerning trend—a shift toward a more authoritarian world order. This trend begs the question of whether traditionally more democratic BRICS countries, such as India and South Africa, are committed to upholding democratic values while engaging with increasingly authoritarian partners within the alliance.

The challenges posed by Indonesia's rejection underscore the urgent need for BRICS to confront the contradictions within its ranks. The alliance faces a critical choice—whether to prioritise unity at the expense of democratic values or seek common ground that aligns with the principles of freedom and human rights. The path it chooses will determine its credibility and effectiveness as a global player.

Moreover, Indonesia's rejection should serve as a cautionary tale for BRICS as it considers future expansions. It highlights the importance of a thoughtful and strategic approach to membership, one that takes into account not only economic considerations but also shared values and geopolitical alignment. Rushing to include new members without due diligence and consensus-building can lead to internal tensions and undermine the alliance's cohesiveness.

In conclusion, Indonesia's refusal to join BRICS is not just a missed opportunity for the alliance but a reflection of the complex geopolitical landscape and diverging priorities among its members. BRICS must grapple with these challenges head-on and make informed decisions about its future direction, governance, and principles. Its ability to navigate these complexities will determine its role in shaping the global order and promoting a world that upholds democratic values and human rights, but the path forward remains uncertain and fraught with challenges.

CHAPTER 17

The Moroccan Debacle

The minor diplomatic crisis that unfolded in 2023 due to South Africa's declaration of Morocco's BRICS application highlighted the communication and coordination challenges within the BRICS alliance. This incident took both the Moroccan leadership and citizens by surprise, as Morocco had no intention of joining BRICS. Instead, they viewed South Africa's announcement as a unilateral move aimed at dictating Moroccan foreign policy and infringing on their sovereignty.

For South Africa, this episode was an embarrassing twist that underscored the need for better internal communication and coordination among BRICS member nations. It also revealed underlying disputes between South Africa and Morocco, particularly concerning South African support for policies that ran counter to Moroccan geopolitical interests, namely in the case of the mineral-rich disputed territory of Western Sahara.

While this diplomatic misstep may appear relatively minor in the broader context of global geopolitics, it underscored the intricate complexities within multinational alliances like BRICS. Such alliances must navigate a delicate balance between their members' individual interests and the collective pursuit of common goals, particularly in an era marked by shifting global power dynamics and emerging challenges.

To successfully navigate these challenges, the BRICS alliance must prioritise effective communication, consensus-building, and conflict resolution mechanisms. Only through robust internal coordination can BRICS harness its economic and geopolitical potential while avoiding inadvertent diplomatic blunders that may undermine its credibility on the international stage.

However, South Africa's role in this incident raises concerns about its prominent position within BRICS. The fact that such a significant misunderstanding could occur under South Africa's watch highlights a potential lack of diplomatic finesse and strategic acumen within the alliance's largest economy. This raises questions about South Africa's ability to effectively guide BRICS in the face of complex geopolitical challenges.

In conclusion, the incident with Morocco should serve as a wake-up call for BRICS. While it may have been a relatively minor incident, it highlights the broader challenges the alliance faces. BRICS can capitalise on its potential as a formidable economic bloc and a diplomatic force, but doing so requires overcoming internal hurdles, fostering unity, and embracing effective communication and diplomacy. Ultimately, the alliance's ability to evolve and adapt in an ever-changing global landscape will determine its long-term impact and relevance on the world stage.

CHAPTER 18

Beyond BRICS+

It's worth noting that a total of 14 countries, excluding the six new members, have submitted applications for permanent BRICS membership. While it's likely that not all of these applicants will ultimately secure a seat within this alliance, these applications offer a glimpse into the trajectory of this economic bloc. To be considered as potential members of this group, each of these 14 nations requires the backing of at least one of the five permanent BRICS members.

This chapter aims to conduct a comprehensive analysis of these applicant nations and assess how their hypothetical membership would impact the BRICS economic alliance as a whole. In this analysis, we will delve into the key characteristics and qualifications of these applicant countries. Factors such as their economic strength, geopolitical significance, and alignment with BRICS' goals and principles will be thoroughly examined.

As we evaluate each applicant, we will also consider the potential implications of their inclusion on the dynamics within the BRICS alliance. Will their membership enhance the alliance's economic power and geopolitical influence, or could it potentially introduce conflicts and challenges? These are critical questions that must be addressed.

Furthermore, we will explore any existing relationships or partnerships that these applicant countries have with the current BRICS members. Such partnerships can provide valuable insights into why a specific country is seeking BRICS membership and how it might contribute to the alliance.

In addition to the applicant nations' qualifications and potential contributions, we will examine the benefits and drawbacks of their membership, both for the applicant nation and for the existing BRICS members. This assessment will shed light on whether their inclusion aligns with BRICS' objectives and whether it strengthens or dilutes the alliance's identity and mission.

Bangladesh:

In a manner akin to the newly admitted members of the BRICS + alliance, Egypt and the UAE, Bangladesh holds a minority stake in the New Development Bank. Furthermore, Bangladesh boasts robust economic ties with the two Asian members of the original "big 4" BRICS nations, in addition to sharing historical and cultural connections with its BRICS neighbour, India. It is evident that Bangladesh has consistently stood out as one of the most promising economies on the Asian continent.

These compelling factors are likely to have exerted a significant influence on Bangladesh's decision to seek membership within the BRICS alliance. Indeed, there is strong evidence to suggest that Bangladesh initiated its application process in early 2023, raising expectations that it will be included in the alliance during its next expansion.

The impending inclusion of Bangladesh is poised to bring noteworthy implications for both the nation itself and the existing BRICS members. For Bangladesh, BRICS membership could offer enhanced economic opportunities, access to resources, and avenues for bolstering its diplomatic standing on the global stage. It aligns with the country's ambition to further solidify its position as a key player in the Asian and international arenas.

From the perspective of the BRICS alliance, Bangladesh's accession expands the alliance's footprint in South Asia, strengthens its economic prowess, and deepens its engagement with strategically vital regions. It signifies a concerted effort by BRICS to broaden its reach and influence across the Asian continent.

However, as BRICS continues to evolve and expand, the alliance faces the challenge of harmonising diverse interests and objectives among its member states. Bangladesh's entry, while promising, will necessitate careful navigation of geopolitical complexities, economic alignments, and diplomatic intricacies within the alliance.

In conclusion, Bangladesh's prospective membership in the BRICS alliance underscores the shifting dynamics of global geopolitics and economics. As the alliance expands and diversifies, it must confront both opportunities and challenges, striving to balance the interests of its member nations while presenting a unified front on the international stage.

Algeria:

Algeria's application for BRICS membership in 2022, with strong indications of its official inclusion in the alliance during the next expansion, raises intriguing questions about the underlying motivations. While on the surface, this move may appear perplexing, it is possible to speculate about the Algerian leadership's strategic considerations.

One plausible, albeit somewhat disconcerting interpretation, is that Algeria sees the BRICS alliance as a potential support network in its enduring regional rivalry with Morocco. Algeria's alignment with Russia and China on the international stage, in stark contrast to Morocco's close relationship with the United States, may have contributed to this decision. If this speculation holds true, it could cast the BRICS alliance in the light of being an "anti-Western" bloc, which has the potential to strain its public image, particularly in the eyes of Western nations.

The dynamics between Algeria and Morocco have been marked by long-standing disputes and intense competition for regional influence. In this context, Algeria's inclination to join BRICS could be seen as a strategic manoeuvre to counterbalance Morocco's alliances and secure support from major global players aligned with BRICS.

However, from the perspective of BRICS, Algeria's inclusion represents a significant expansion into North Africa and strengthens the alliance's geopolitical reach. It underscores BRICS' evolving role in global politics and its appeal to nations seeking to diversify their diplomatic and economic partnerships.

Nonetheless, the perceived anti-Western stance associated with Algeria's membership may present daunting diplomatic challenges for BRICS. Balancing relationships with Western powers while accommodating new members with differing orientations is a precarious tightrope that the alliance will need to navigate adeptly.

In conclusion, Algeria's prospective membership in BRICS adds an intriguing yet potentially unsettling dimension to the alliance's growth and influence. It highlights the complex web of geopolitical rivalries and strategic alignments in the international arena. As BRICS expands, it must carefully manage its image and diplomatic relations in an increasingly polarised world.

Bahrain & Kuwait:

Both Bahrain and Kuwait, two relatively small nations in the Middle East, submitted formal applications to join the BRICS bloc in 2023. The decision to pursue BRICS+ membership may be strongly influenced by the recent inclusion of their larger neighbours and fellow GCC partners in the BRICS alliance. This development suggests a potentially significant shift in the economic and geopolitical trajectory of the GCC economic bloc as a whole.

For these Gulf nations, joining BRICS+ could represent an opportunity to diversify their economic partnerships and reduce dependence on traditional Western allies. The inclusion of Saudi Arabia and the United Arab Emirates in BRICS likely played a pivotal role in motivating Bahrain and Kuwait to explore this avenue.

In particular, the GCC countries may view BRICS+ as a platform to strengthen ties with major global players like Russia and China, both of which have exhibited a growing interest in the Middle East. This strategic move aligns with a broader trend of nations in the region seeking to broaden their economic and diplomatic horizons.

However, this shift may also introduce complexities and challenges. As Bahrain and Kuwait potentially become part of BRICS+, they will need to navigate their existing partnerships and alliances, particularly with Western powers. This could result in a delicate balancing act between their long-standing relationships and their emerging ties within the BRICS framework.

Moreover, the inclusion of Bahrain and Kuwait in BRICS+ highlights the alliance's expansion into the Middle East, further emphasising its global reach and ambitions. It underscores

BRICS+ as a platform that attracts nations seeking alternative economic and geopolitical pathways in a rapidly evolving world order.

In conclusion, Bahrain's and Kuwait's applications to join BRICS + reflect a broader trend of Middle Eastern nations diversifying their economic and diplomatic partnerships. While this move could offer new opportunities, it also presents challenges in terms of balancing existing alliances and navigating the complex web of international politics. As BRICS+ continues to evolve and expand, it solidifies its position as a significant player on the global stage.

Palestine:

Palestine's application to join the BRICS bloc in 2023 raises serious questions about the alliance's evolving direction, and its approach to potential new members seems increasingly misguided. This move by Palestine, a nation with an unstable economy and limited global recognition, underscores the notion that BRICS has shifted away from its initial economic focus and is becoming entangled in a web of geopolitical considerations that could have far-reaching and detrimental implications.

By entertaining the possibility of Palestine's membership, BRICS risks not only straining but severely damaging its already complex and sensitive relationship with Israel. It's essential to emphasise that Israel views the Gaza Strip, controlled by Hamas, as a hotbed of terrorism and a significant security threat. BRICS' willingness to engage with Palestine could be interpreted as a tacit endorsement of a region that Israel views as a terrorist haven.

This engagement with Palestine could indeed draw the BRICS bloc into the intricate web of Palestine's internal disputes, which are marked by fragmentation and occasional violent conflicts among various Palestinian factions. Such entanglement is detrimental to the alliance's stability and credibility, raising concerns about its ability to maintain its original economic objectives.

The Palestinian leadership may indeed view BRICS membership as a strategic move to gain international recognition and influential allies in its ongoing conflict with Israel. However, from a purely logical perspective, BRICS stands to gain very little by admitting Palestine into its once-exclusive club. Instead, it risks compromising its standing on the global stage by being perceived as supportive of entities that Israel considers security threats.

Furthermore, the consideration of Palestine's membership could be seen as an attempt by the more established BRICS members to curry favour with their newer Arab counterparts and potential applicants. This diplomatic manoeuvre could be part of a broader strategy to strengthen ties with Arab nations within the expanded alliance. However, it might come at the cost of alienating Israel, a long-standing and strategic partner for some BRICS members.

It's worth noting that Iran, one of the newer members of BRICS +, has a history of tense and hostile relations with Israel. Iran has been a vocal supporter of Palestinian causes and has backed radical groups like Hamas, which directly opposes Israel. By considering Palestine's membership, BRICS may inadvertently align itself more closely with Iran's stance on the Israeli-Palestinian conflict, further straining relations with Israel.

In conclusion, Palestine's application to join BRICS reflects a disconcerting shift in the alliance's focus from purely economic matters to more complex and potentially damaging geopolitical considerations. While it may serve certain diplomatic interests, BRICS must critically assess the potential consequences of such a move, particularly regarding its relationship with Israel and the risks associated with embracing regions that are viewed as threats to international security. The alliance's ability to balance its original economic objectives with these evolving geopolitical complexities will determine its long-term effectiveness and reputation on the global stage.

Belarus:

Belarus's 2023 application to join the BRICS+ bloc is a perplexing development that raises serious questions about the alliance's direction and priorities. Belarus, often referred to as the "Last Dictatorship in Europe," and widely seen as a Russian proxy, stands in stark contrast to the typical profile of a BRICS member. It lacks a robust economy, a significant population, and suffers from an international reputation akin to that of a pariah state, not dissimilar to Russia itself.

From a purely logical standpoint, Belarus appears to be more of a liability than an asset for BRICS. Its inclusion seems at odds with the alliance's original mission and objectives. Belarus's application, with Russia's support, suggests a deviation from the alliance's economic focus and an inclination towards geopolitics, as Belarus's economic contribution is arguably nominal.

The strong backing of Belarus's membership by Russia, BRICS' largest economy, suggests that this move may be part of Russia's strategy to consolidate power within the alliance. This is particularly significant in the face of growing international pressure and sanctions against Russia. By expanding its sphere of influence within BRICS, Russia may be seeking to offset its diminishing global influence and isolation on the international stage.

However, this Russia-centric approach is not without consequences. It further isolates BRICS from other nations and reinforces the perception that the alliance is primarily an anti-Western bloc. This, in turn, could hinder BRICS' ability to engage in constructive global diplomacy and cooperation, as its actions may be viewed as serving the interests of a select few rather than the broader international community.

In conclusion, Belarus's application to join the BRICS+ bloc, under Russia's auspices, reflects a concerning shift within the alliance. While it may serve Russia's short-term interests, it raises doubts about BRICS' commitment to its original economic goals and its ability to maintain a balanced and inclusive approach to global affairs. The alliance must carefully consider the long-term implications of such a move, particularly regarding its international reputation and its capacity to foster meaningful cooperation on a global scale.

Kazakhstan:

Kazakhstan's 2023 application to join BRICS marks an intriguing development for both the country and the alliance. As a landlocked nation, Kazakhstan's motivation likely stems from its desire to diversify its list of trading partners and strengthen its economic ties with a diverse range of nations.

Kazakhstan's geographical location makes it particularly keen on seeking partnerships that can enhance its economic growth and reduce its dependence on a limited set of neighbouring countries. Joining BRICS would offer Kazakhstan the opportunity to engage with a broader spectrum of emerging economies and expand its trade networks.

Moreover, Kazakhstan's application may be influenced by the observed trend within BRICS of being relatively less critical of factors like human rights and democratic values among its members. This aligns with the preferences of Kazakhstan's ruling class, which may view BRICS as a platform where they can interact with like-minded nations that prioritise economic development over political or social issues.

Kazakhstan's potential inclusion in BRICS raises questions about the alliance's evolving identity and priorities. While the original mission of BRICS was primarily economic, the inclusion of countries like Kazakhstan suggests a broader geopolitical role. This expansion may impact the alliance's dynamics, with economic and political considerations coming into play.

For Kazakhstan, BRICS membership could open up new avenues for economic growth and diversification. However, it's essential for both the country and the alliance to carefully consider the implications of this expansion, balancing economic opportunities with potential challenges to the alliance's cohesion and its original vision. The coming years will reveal how Kazakhstan's BRICS membership may influence the trajectory of this influential economic and political bloc.

Vietnam:

Vietnam's 2023 application to join BRICS reflects a strategic move by the country to enhance its economic prospects and build stronger relationships with other nations. Vietnam's rapid economic growth and its pursuit of a dynamic and diversified economy could benefit significantly from BRICS membership. Joining BRICS would offer Vietnam the opportunity to collaborate with a diverse group of emerging economies, access new markets, and foster economic development.

Furthermore, Vietnam's application might be influenced by its desire to utilise BRICS as a diplomatic channel for addressing long-standing border disputes with its larger neighbour, China. The complex history of disputes and conflicts between Vietnam and China spans millennia, and BRICS could serve as an initial platform for diplomatic engagement and discussion on these matters.

This move by Vietnam aligns with the evolving role of BRICS, which has expanded its focus beyond solely economic matters to encompass broader geopolitical and diplomatic considerations. While BRICS began primarily as an economic alliance, the inclusion of nations like Vietnam suggests a growing interest in addressing political and territorial issues within the group.

Vietnam's potential inclusion in BRICS highlights the evolving dynamics and objectives of the alliance. The entry of a rapidly growing Southeast Asian nation underscores BRICS' reach beyond its original scope and mission. As Vietnam's application progresses, it will be interesting to observe how the alliance navigates the intricate balance between economic cooperation and addressing political issues that have the potential to shape the geopolitical landscape in the coming years.

Thailand:

Thailand's application to join the expanded BRICS bloc in 2023 appears to be primarily motivated by economic interests. The country has historically maintained relatively decent relations with most of the BRICS member nations, and this lack of strong binding treaties or alliances with these countries suggests that their interest in joining BRICS is predominantly driven by economic considerations.

Thailand, as a member of an expanded BRICS group, would likely aim to leverage this alliance for economic growth and diversification. BRICS membership would provide Thailand with opportunities to engage in trade and economic cooperation with some of the world's emerging economic powerhouses. By expanding its network of economic partners, Thailand can potentially bolster its own economy, stimulate trade, and attract investments from the BRICS nations.

Furthermore, Thailand's application to join BRICS aligns with the alliance's broader evolution. While BRICS was initially formed as an economic bloc, it has increasingly broadened its focus to include diplomatic and geopolitical matters. Thailand's involvement could contribute to this diplomatic expansion while strengthening the bloc's economic ties.

Thailand's application underscores the growing relevance and appeal of BRICS as a platform for fostering economic partnerships and addressing broader geopolitical challenges. As this application progresses, it will be intriguing to see how Thailand's inclusion could influence the alliance's dynamics and objectives, particularly in the realm of economic cooperation.

Cuba:

Cuba's application for BRICS membership in 2023 raises several complex issues and potential consequences. The Cuban leadership, confronted with international isolation, economic challenges, and sanctions, could indeed view BRICS membership as a means to address some of these problems and circumvent existing sanctions.

From the Cuban perspective, joining BRICS, especially with Russia's support, might provide a lifeline to help improve their struggling economy. It could potentially open up trade and economic cooperation with the BRICS nations, thereby reducing the economic pressures and isolation that Cuba faces due to its international pariah status.

Furthermore, the historical connection between Cuba and Russia, dating back to the days of the Soviet Union, could be a driving force behind this move. Russia may see a Cuban BRICS membership as an opportunity to strengthen its influence in the Caribbean and use Cuba as a pawn in its geopolitical strategy, particularly in countering U.S. attempts to normalise relations with the island nation.

However, from a broader perspective, Cuba's inclusion in BRICS is more of a long-term liability than an asset for the alliance as a whole. Cuba doesn't bring significant economic or geopolitical advantages to BRICS. Its rogue state status, expansionist Marxist ideology, and contentious international relations have made it one of the most sanctioned countries globally. While Russia may see value in Cuban membership for its own interests, it could further isolate BRICS and strain its relations with other powerful nations.

Cuba's potential inclusion in BRICS will undoubtedly spark debate and scrutiny, both within the alliance and on the international stage. It remains to be seen how this move will impact BRICS' dynamics and reputation in the evolving global order.

Honduras:

Honduras, in many ways, could be considered a relatively small economy, especially when compared to the more established BRICS members. One important statistic that puts Honduras on the map, albeit in a macabre manner, would be the fact that it has the second-highest murder rate in the world (with BRICS member, South Africa, having the third highest).

The Honduran leadership would have viewed its 2023 BRICS application as a potential channel by which they can secure financial support for their economy, which is in quite an unstable situation. The country faces significant economic challenges, and joining BRICS might provide a much-needed economic lifeline.

However, while Honduras might stand to gain from BRICS membership, the existing bloc might get little to no benefit from granting Honduras membership. The tiny Central American nation's uncontrollable crime rates and the autocratic steps taken by the government to combat crime make it more of a liability than an asset. Honduras' inclusion would not significantly enhance the economic or geopolitical strength of BRICS and could potentially draw negative attention to the alliance due to the country's concerning crime rates and governance issues.

It remains to be seen how BRICS will approach Honduras' application and whether the alliance will consider the potential risks and benefits of admitting a nation facing such complex challenges into its fold.

Senegal:

Senegal's 2023 application to join the expanded BRICS+ economic bloc appears to be primarily motivated by its strong economic ties with existing BRICS members, particularly India and China. Senegal has established itself as a significant trading partner with India and China, with the latter being its largest import partner, accounting for more than 20% of its imports. Additionally, India and Russia play crucial roles as import partners for Senegal.

The larger BRICS members likely view Senegal's application as an opportunity to further solidify their already strong economic relationships with the West African nation and maintain a strategic foothold in the region.

However, it is important to note that Senegal does not possess the economic prowess or population size traditionally associated with BRICS nations, especially when adhering to the original BRIC acronym. This raises questions about whether Senegal's inclusion aligns with the core characteristics that defined BRICS when the alliance was first conceived.

Senegal's application presents an interesting dynamic within the BRICS+ expansion, where nations with varying economic scales seek to join the bloc. The move reflects the changing global economic landscape and the alliance's willingness to consider new members based on their economic contributions and strategic value rather than solely adhering to the original BRIC criteria. It remains to be seen how the existing BRICS members will evaluate Senegal's application and the implications it holds for the alliance's future.

Venezuela:

Venezuela, often seen as the poster child for an unstable nation, grapples with a multitude of challenges, including international sanctions, historically high inflation numbers, political instability, and rising poverty rates. To comprehend Venezuela's predicament, it's essential to delve into its complex history and current disputes with the Western world.

Venezuela's modern history is marked by a series of political and economic shifts. It enjoyed periods of relative stability and prosperity, primarily driven by its vast oil reserves, making it one of the world's leading oil exporters in the mid-20th century. However, political turmoil and social inequality simmered beneath the surface. Decades of political corruption, authoritarian rule, and an over-reliance on oil revenue left the country's institutions weak and its economy vulnerable to global oil price fluctuations.

In the late 1990s, Hugo Chávez, a charismatic military officer, won the presidency through democratic elections and launched the Bolivarian Revolution, which aimed to reduce social inequality and increase the state's control over the economy. His policies were characterised by land reform, wealth redistribution, and nationalisation of key industries, including the oil sector.

While Chávez's rule enjoyed popular support from many Venezuelans, it also led to economic mismanagement, corruption, and the erosion of democratic norms. Chávez's successor, Nicolás Maduro, continued these policies and faced allegations of authoritarianism and electoral irregularities.

Venezuela's domestic challenges have been compounded by international disputes, especially with the Western world. Accusations of human rights abuses, suppression of political opposition, and a questionable electoral process have led to sanctions imposed by Western nations, particularly the United States and the European Union. These sanctions have targeted key individuals and institutions within the Maduro government and have significantly impacted the country's economy.

Venezuela's application to join the BRICS+ bloc in 2023 can be viewed as an act of desperation to improve its economic situation. Its vast oil reserves are a critical asset that many BRICS nations covet. However, this move raises complex questions about how the BRICS alliance will engage with a nation led by a regime that is a subject of international concern and sanctions.

In the context of BRICS, the inclusion of Venezuela could further strain the alliance's relations with the West and exacerbate concerns about BRICS being a safe haven for autocratic regimes.

Bolivia:

Bolivia's 2023 application to join BRICS represents a significant shift in its foreign policy, considering its relative isolationism from international alliances and economic blocs. While Bolivia's inclusion could be seen as a departure from its previous stance, it does raise questions about what this South American nation brings to the BRICS collective.

From an objective standpoint, Bolivia doesn't offer much to the BRICS alliance in terms of economic prowess, military power projection potential, or a significant population. It's a landlocked country with unique social, political, and economic circumstances that may not align with the established BRICS members. However, these apparent limitations could be viewed differently by the larger BRICS members.

The BRICS nations, especially those with a significant demand for natural resources, might see Bolivia as an opportunity. Given the current state of its government and relatively lax regulatory procedures, there could be an interest in exploiting Bolivia's rich natural resources. The nation is known for its reserves of minerals like lithium, which is in high demand for the production of batteries for electric vehicles and renewable energy storage. Bolivia's vast reserves of natural gas and other minerals could also be of interest to BRICS members.

Bolivia's application introduces complex questions about how the alliance will engage with a nation that brings unique opportunities and challenges. It remains to be seen how this potential expansion will impact BRICS' dynamics and its pursuit of common goals in an evolving global landscape.

CHAPTER 19

Aspiring BRICS+ Members

The prospect of further expansion of the BRICS+ alliance in the coming years has garnered considerable interest from various nations. While the BRICS leadership has indicated a series of expansions, smaller nations and economies see this as an opportunity to apply and potentially join. For these applicant nations, BRICS represents a channel through which they can enhance their relationships with the existing BRICS members, both economically and diplomatically.

However, the enthusiasm for expanding BRICS also comes with some concerns. Notably, several rogue nations and autocratic dictatorships have expressed interest in joining BRICS. This includes countries like North Korea, Myanmar, and Syria, all of which have contentious international reputations. The prospect of such nations becoming part of BRICS raises questions about the alliance's direction and its perception on the global stage.

This interest from less democratic and more authoritarian countries could contribute to the growing perception that BRICS is evolving into an openly anti-Western alliance. Such a perception may not bode well for the alliance in the long term, as it could strain individual member's relationships with Western nations. While there may be political factions within

BRICS member nations with an active interest in disrupting relations with the West, a delicate balance is needed to maintain the alliance's global standing while accommodating new members. The expansion of BRICS+ brings both opportunities and challenges, and it remains to be seen how the alliance will navigate this complex landscape in the future.

In conclusion, the recent developments within the BRICS + alliance reflect a critical juncture in the evolution of this economic bloc. What began as an academic hypothetical regarding a group of developing economies has transformed into an unlikely alliance of rising nations. BRICS now faces an unprecedented choice, one that will shape the values and principles of this bloc for generations to come.

The alliance must grapple with a fundamental decision: will it uphold the ideals upon which modern civilization is built, including democracy, human rights, and respect for international norms, or will it be enticed by short-term gains and succumb to the allure of autocratic regimes? This choice will define the trajectory and global impact of BRICS as it navigates a complex and ever-changing geopolitical landscape.

The challenge for BRICS is to strike a balance between pursuing its economic and geopolitical interests while maintaining its commitment to the core principles of democracy, human rights, and international cooperation. How the alliance addresses this challenge will ultimately determine its role in shaping the future of the global order and its standing on the world stage. The decisions made by BRICS in the coming years will have far-reaching implications, not only for the alliance itself but for the broader international community.

REFERENCES

Chapter 1:

Goldman Sachs | Commemorates 150 Year History - With GS Research Report (2014). Goldman Sachs | Commemorates 150 Year History - With GS Research Report,. [online] Goldman Sachs. Available at: https://www.goldmansachs.com/our-firm/history/moments/2001-brics.html.

Bishop, M. (2022). The BRICS countries: Where Next and What Impact on the Global Economy? [online] Economics Observatory. Available at: https://www.economicsobservatory.com/the-brics-countries-where-next-and-what-impact-on-the-global-economy.

Ortega, A. (2014). BRIC nationalism. [online] Elcano Royal Institute. Available at: https://www.realinstitutoelcano.org/en/blog/global-spectator-bric-nationalism/.

Who You Calling a BRIC? (2013). Bloomberg.com. [online] 12 Nov. Available at: https://www.bloomberg.com/view/articles/2013-11-12/who-you-calling-a-bric-.

Stuenkel, O., 2020. The BRICS and the future of global order. Lexington books.

Pant, H.V., 2013. The BRICS fallacy. The Washington Quarterly, 36(3), pp.91-105.

Chapter 2:

web.archive.org. (2015). Information about BRICS. [online] Available at: https://web.archive.org/web/20150710163822/http://brics6.itamaraty.gov.br/about-brics/information-about-brics.

Nations eye stable reserve system. (2009). news.bbc.co.uk. [online] 16 Jun. Available at: http://news.bbc.co.uk/2/hi/business/8102216.stm.

UPDATE 6-BRIC demands more clout, steers clear of dollar talk. (2009). Reuters. [online] 16 Jun. Available at: https://www.reuters.com/article/marketsNews/idUSLG67435120090616.

Kramer, A.E. (2009). Emerging Economies Meet in Russia. The New York Times. [online] 16 Jun. Available at: https://www.nytimes.com/2009/06/17/world/europe/17bric.html?ref=business.

Brookings. (n.d.). The U.S. Financial and Economic Crisis: Where Does It Stand and Where Do We Go From Here? [online] Available at: https://www.brookings.edu/articles/the-u-s-financial-and-economic-crisis-where-does-it-stand-and-where-do-we-go-from-here/ [Accessed 28 Oct. 2023].

Welle (www.dw.com), D. (n.d.). First BRIC summit concludes | DW | 16.06.2009. [online] DW.COM. Available at: https://www.dw.com/en/first-bric-summit-concludes/a-4335954.

Das Gupta, A. and Luthi, L.M. (2016). The Sino-Indian war of 1962 : new perspectives. London: Routledge.

Noorani, A.G. (2010). India–China Boundary Problem 1846–1947. Oxford University Press.

Sectsco.org. (2017). Shanghai Cooperation Organisation | SCO. [online] Available at: http://eng.sectsco.org/about_sco/20170109/190857.html.

Chapter 3:

Smith, Jack A. (2011). BRIC Becomes BRICS: Changes on the Geopolitical Chessboard. Foreign Policy Journal [online] Available at: https://www.foreignpolicyjournal.com/2011/01/21/bric-becomes-brics-changes-on-the-geopolitical-chessboard/2/

The Indian Express. (2011). BRICS should coordinate in key areas of development: PM. [online] Available at: https://indianexpress.com/article/india/latest-news/brics-should-coordinate-in-key-areas-of-development-pm/.

Van Mead, N. (2018). China in Africa: win-win development, or a New colonialism? [online] The Guardian. Available at: https://www.theguardian.com/cities/2018/jul/31/china-in-africa-win-win-development-or-a-new-colonialism.

Sharma, N. (2023). China in Africa: Soft Power and the Development of Neocolonial States. Cornell Undergraduate Research Journal, [online] 2(1), pp.75–85. doi:https://doi.org/10.37513/curj.v2i1.716.

Chapter 4:

web.archive.org. (2013). Russia says BRICS eye joint anti-crisis fund | Reuters. [online] Available at: https://web.archive.org/web/20130515075723/http://in.reuters.com/article/2012/06/21/russia-brics-imf-idINDEE85K04C20120621.

web.archive.org. (2013). India sees BRICS development bank agreed by 2014 summit | Reuters. [online] Available at: https://web.archive.org/web/20130528093058/http://in.reuters.com/article/2013/04/19/g20-brics-india-idINDEE93I0DK20130419.

www.ft.com. (n.d.). Putin was ready to put nuclear weapons on alert in Crimea crisis. Financial Times. [online]

Available at: https://www.ft.com/content/41873ed2-
cb60-11e4-8ad9-00144feab7de.

www.uawarexplained.com. (n.d.). Annexation of Crimea
| Ukraine War Explained. [online] Available at: https://
www.uawarexplained.com/annexation-of-crimea/?version=sixty-
minutes.

web.archive.org. (2014). BRICS may decide on $100 billion fund
early 2014 - Russia | Reuters. [online] Available at: https://
web.archive.org/web/20140201194824/http://in.reuters.com/
article/2013/10/11/g20-brics-fund-idINL6N0I13N720131011.

Chapter 5:

brics2021.gov.in. (n.d.). BRICS INDIA 2021 | Ministry of External
Affairs. [online] Available at: https://brics2021.gov.in/games.

english.news.cn. (n.d.). 2022 BRICS Games opens online-Xinhua.
[online] Available at: https://english.news.cn/20220901/
de178738fdf8442bbf2a4764ba4c54aa/c.html.

Chapter 6:

thediplomat.com. (n.d.). A Fiber-Optic Silk Road. [online] Available
at: https://thediplomat.com/2015/04/a-fiber-optic-silk-road/.

The BRICS Post. (n.d.). Brazil-Europe Internet cable to cost $185
million. [online] Available at: https://www.thebricspost.com/
brazil-europe-internet-cable-to-cost-185-million/.

The Henry M. Jackson School of International Studies. (2016).
International Reactions to U.S. Cybersecurity Policy: The BRICS
undersea cable. [online] Available at: https://jsis.washington.edu/
news/reactions-u-s-cybersecurity-policy-bric-undersea-cable/.

Chapter 7:

Ibge.gov.br. (2015). BRICS. [online] Available at: https://brics.ibge.gov.br/publicacao.html.

Chapter 8:

Shan, L.Y. (2023). Western sanctions on Russia could push the BRICS alliance closer. [online] CNBC. Available at: https://www.cnbc.com/2023/09/11/western-sanctions-on-russia-could-push-the-brics-alliance-closer-appec.html.

Salzman, R.S. (2019). Russia, BRICS, and the Disruption of Global Order. doi:https://doi.org/10.2307/j.ctvcj2sb2.

Brown, D. (2022). Ukraine invasion: Russia's attack in maps. BBC News. [online] 24 Feb. Available at: https://www.bbc.com/news/world-europe-60506682.

Mediazona. (n.d.). Russian casualties in Ukraine. Mediazona count, updated. [online] Available at: https://en.zona.media/article/2022/05/20/casualties_eng.

Ukraine-Russia News. (2023). The New York Times. [online] Available at: https://www.nytimes.com/news-event/ukraine-russia.

Center for Preventive Action (2023). Conflict in Ukraine. [online] Global Conflict Tracker. Available at: https://www.cfr.org/global-conflict-tracker/conflict/conflict-ukraine.

Walker, N. (2023). Conflict in Ukraine: A timeline (2014 – eve of 2022 invasion). [online] UK Parliament . Available at: https://commonslibrary.parliament.uk/research-briefings/cbp-9476/.

Ministry of Foreign Affairs of Ukraine (2019). 10 facts you should know about Russian military aggression against ukraine. [online] mfa.gov.ua. Available at: https://mfa.gov.ua/en/10-facts-you-should-know-about-russian-military-aggression-against-ukraine.

Al-Hlou, Y., Froliak, M., Khavin, D., Koettl, C., Willis, H., Cardia, A., Reneau, N. and Browne, M. (2022). Caught on Camera, Traced by Phone: The Russian Military Unit That Killed Dozens in Bucha. The New York Times. [online] 22 Dec. Available at: https://www.nytimes.com/2022/12/22/video/russia-ukraine-bucha-massacre-takeaways.html.

Shuster, S. (2022). The Crime Scene Left Behind at a Summer Camp in Bucha. [online] Time. Available at: https://time.com/6166681/bucha-massacre-ukraine-dispatch/.

India Today. (n.d.). Kim Jong Un to visit Russia's Pacific fleet amid talk of arms alliance. [online] Available at: https://www.indiatoday.in/world/story/north-korea-kim-jong-un-visits-russia-pacific-fleet-arms-deal-buzz-2436401-2023-09-16.

Srinivas, J., 2022. Russia and China in BRICS: Convergences and Divergences. In Future of the BRICS and the Role of Russia and China (pp. 147-192). Singapore: Springer Nature Singapore.

Toloraya, G., 2015. Why does Russia need BRICS. Russia in Global Affairs, 19.

Lukyanov, F., 2013. Russia in BRICS: substantial or instrumental partnership?. Laying the BRICS of a New Global Order: From Yekaterinburg 2009 to eThekwini 2013, p.119.

Michailova, S., McCarthy, D.J. and Puffer, S.M., 2013. Russia: as solid as a BRIC?. Critical perspectives on international business, 9(1/2), pp.5-18.

Chapter 9:

BBC News (2023). Why Is the South China Sea contentious? BBC News. [online] 12 Jul. Available at: https://www.bbc.com/news/world-asia-pacific-13748349.

Center for Preventive Action (2023). Territorial Disputes in the

South China Sea. [online] Global Conflict Tracker. Available at: https://www.cfr.org/global-conflict-tracker/conflict/territorial-disputes-south-china-sea.

Michael Patrick Cullinane (2017). Open Door Era. Edinburgh University Press.

Gries, P.H. (2004). China's new nationalism : pride, politics, and diplomacy. Berkeley Calif. ; London: University Of California Press.

BBC (2022). India-China Border Dispute Explained in 400 Words. BBC News. [online] 14 Dec. Available at: https://www.bbc.com/news/world-asia-53062484.

Ryan, M.A., Finkelstein, D.M., McDevitt, M.A. and CNA Corporation (2016). Chinese Warfighting: The PLA Experience since 1949. Routledge.

Margolis, E. (2004). War at the Top of the World. Routledge.

Feige, C. and Miron, J.A. (2008). The opium wars, opium legalization and opium consumption in China. Applied Economics Letters, 15(12), pp.911–913. doi:https://doi.org/10.1080/13504850600972295.

Chen, S. (2017). Merchants of War and Peace. [online] doi:https://doi.org/10.5790/hongkong/9789888390564.001.0001.

Waters, D. (1991). The Re—Occupation of Hong Kong in August 1945. Journal of the Hong Kong Branch of the Royal Asiatic Society, [online] 31, pp.201–204. Available at: https://www.jstor.org/stable/23891036 .

Drea, E. (2006). Introductory Essays on Researching Japanese War Crimes Records. [online] Available at: https://www.archives.gov/files/iwg/japanese-war-crimes/introductory-essays.pdf.
Chan, C., Dao, A., Hou, J., Jin, T. and Tuong, C. (2011). China's Great Firewall. [online] cs.stanford.edu. Available at: https://cs.stanford.edu/people/eroberts/cs181/projects/2010-11/FreeExpressionVsSocialCohesion/china_policy.html.

The Great Firewall of China. (2017). Bloomberg.com. [online] 13 Oct. Available at: https://www.bloomberg.com/view/quicktake/ great-firewall-of-china.

Rogin, J. (n.d.). Opinion | China's atrocities in Tibet are growing too big to ignore. Washington Post. [online] Available at: https:// www.washingtonpost.com/opinions/global-opinions/chinas- atrocities-in-tibet-are-growing-too-big-to-ignore/2020/12/24/ ba9d5c4e-4624-11eb-b0e4-0f182923a025_story.html.

Holden, K. (2015). China's Crackdowns in Tibet. [online] The Diplomat. Available at: https://thediplomat.com/2015/04/chinas- crackdowns-in-tibet.

Anon, (2023). UN Member Countries Condemn China's Crimes Against Humanity | Human Rights Watch. [online] Available at: https://www.hrw.org/news/2023/10/23/un-member- countries-condemn-chinas-crimes-against-humanity#:~:text=UN %20Member%20Countries%20Condemn%20China.

Maizland, L. (2022). China's Repression of Uyghurs in Xinjiang. [online] Council on Foreign Relations. Available at: https:// www.cfr.org/backgrounder/china-xinjiang-uyghurs-muslims- repression-genocide-human-rights.

BBC (2022). Who Are the Uyghurs and Why Is China Being Accused of Genocide? BBC News. [online] 24 May. Available at: https:// www.bbc.com/news/world-asia-china-22278037.

Kuo, L. (2019). In China, they're closing churches, jailing pastors – and even rewriting scripture. [online] the Guardian. Available at: https://www.theguardian.com/world/2019/jan/13/china- christians-religious-persecution-translation-bible.

The Tablet. (n.d.). Report reveals widespread Christian persecution in China. [online] The Tablet. Available at: https:// www.thetablet.co.uk/news/16668/report-reveals-widespread- christian-persecution-in-china.

The Guardian. (2019). One in three Christians face persecution in Asia, report finds. [online] Available at: https://www.theguardian.com/world/2019/jan/16/one-in-three-christians-face-persecution-in-asia-report-finds.

Glosny, M.A., 2010. China and the BRICs: A real (but limited) partnership in a unipolar world. Polity, 42(1), pp.100-129.

Lukin, A. and Xuesong, F., 2019. What is BRICS for China?. Strategic Analysis, 43(6), pp.620-631.

Katada, S.N., Roberts, C. and Armijo, L.E., 2017. The varieties of collective financial statecraft: the BRICS and China. Political Science Quarterly, 132(3), pp.403-433.

Chapter 10:

Paraguassu, L. (2023). Brazil now main holdout against BRICS expansion, sources say. Reuters. [online] 2 Aug. Available at: https://www.reuters.com/world/brazil-now-main-holdout-against-brics-expansion-sources-say-2023-08-02/.

U.S. Department of state (2019). U.S. Relations With Brazil - United States Department of State. [online] United States Department of State. Available at: https://www.state.gov/u-s-relations-with-brazil/.

Saraiva, M.G. (2017). The Brazil-European Union strategic partnership, from Lula to Dilma Rousseff: a shift of focus. Revista Brasileira de Política Internacional, 60(1). doi:https://doi.org/10.1590/0034-7329201600117.

CEPS. (2023). Brazil is back: Unleashing the potential of EU-Brazil relations. [online] Available at: https://www.ceps.eu/ceps-events/brazil-is-back-unleashing-the-potential-of-eu-brazil-relations/ .

www.hbs.edu. (n.d.). Brazil: Leading the BRICs? - Case - Faculty & Research - Harvard Business School. [online] Available at: https://

www.hbs.edu/faculty/Pages/item.aspx?num=39979.

Wilkinson, D. (2018). No Justice for Horrors of Brazil's Military Dictatorship 50 Years On. [online] Human Rights Watch. Available at: https://www.hrw.org/news/2018/12/13/no-justice-horrors-brazils-military-dictatorship-50-years.

Sotero, P. and Armijo, L.E., 2007. Brazil: To be or not to be a BRIC?. Asian perspective, pp.43-70.

Vieira, Pedro Antonio, and Helton Ricardo Ouriques. "Brazil and the BRICS: The trap of short time." Journal of world-systems research 22, no. 2 (2016): 404-429.

Chapter 11:

AfricaNews (2023). South Africa's economy avoids recession with slim first-quarter growth. [online] Africanews. Available at: https://www.africanews.com/2023/06/06/south-africas-economy-avoids-recession-with-slim-first-quarter-growth//.

Why South Africa's Electricity Crisis Is at the Heart of Its Problems. (2023). Bloomberg.com. [online] 20 May. Available at: https://www.bloomberg.com/news/newsletters/2023-05-20/the-collateral-damage-of-south-africa-s-power-crisis-new-economy-saturday.

S. African Economy Likely in Technical Recession, Citi Says. (2022). Bloomberg.com. [online] 19 Oct. Available at: https://www.bloomberg.com/news/articles/2022-10-19/south-african-economy-likely-in-technical-recession-citi-says#xj4y7vzkg.

Lodge, T. (1998). Political Corruption in South Africa. African Affairs, [online] 97(387), pp.157–187. Available at: https://www.jstor.org/stable/723262.

Cele, S. (2023). Africa's Richest City Is Crumbling Under Chaos and Corruption. Bloomberg.com. [online] 16 Jun. Available at: https://www.bloomberg.com/news/features/2023-06-16/south-africa-s-

crime-chaos-and-corruption-make-it-look-like-a-failed-state.

LODGE, T. (1998). POLITICAL CORRUPTION IN SOUTH AFRICA. African Affairs, 97(387), pp.157–187. doi:https:// doi.org/10.1093/oxfordjournals.afraf.a007924.

AP News. (2023). Putin was meant to be at a summit in South Africa this week. Why was he asked to stay away? [online] Available at: https://apnews.com/article/brics-xi-jinping-putin-china-russia-963108da4d389f8e1e7775c9e002b5f9.

PBS NewsHour. (2023). Putin remotely attends BRICS summit in South Africa while facing war crimes warrant. [online] Available at: https://www.pbs.org/newshour/world/putin-remotely-attends-brics-summit-in-south-africa-while-facing-war-crimes-warrant.

South Africa says inquiry finds no evidence of arms shipment to Russia. (2023). BBC News. [online] 4 Sep. Available at: https:// www.bbc.com/news/world-africa-66703901.

Pradhan, S.K. (2009). The Political Participation And Problems Of People Of Indian Origin In Post-Apartheid South Africa. World Affairs: The Journal of International Issues, [online] 13(1), pp.130–144. Available at: https://www.jstor.org/stable/48505473.

Bruce, D., 2014. Control, discipline and punish?: Addressing corruption in South Africa. South African Crime Quarterly, 48, pp.49-62.

Newham, G., 2002. Tackling police corruption in South Africa. Africa do Sul: Centre for the Study of Violence and reconciliation.

Chapter 12:

Purushothaman, R., 2004. India: realizing BRICs potential. New York, NY: Goldman Sachs.

Stephen, M.D., 2016. India and the BRICS: global bandwagoning and regional balancing. Vestnik RUDN: international relations,

16(4), pp.595-602.

The Wire. (n.d.). As BRICS Evolves Criteria for Expansion, Here's What India Thinks of the 23 Countries That Want to Join. [online] Available at: https://thewire.in/diplomacy/india-brics-23-countries-expansion-stakes.

York, U. of (n.d.). Blog: India - One year after Narendra Modi's re-election, the country's democracy is developing fascistic undertones. [online] University of York. Available at: https://www.york.ac.uk/igdc/news/news/india-developing--fascistic-undertones/.

www.globaltimes.cn. (n.d.). Ultra-nationalism leads India's relations with neighboring countries astray - Global Times. [online] Available at: https://www.globaltimes.cn/content/1192865.shtml.

Jacob, H. (2023). The BRICS test for India's multipolarity rhetoric. The Hindu. [online] 21 Aug. Available at: https://www.thehindu.com/opinion/lead/the-brics-test-for-indias-multipolarity-rhetoric/article67220179.ece.

BABU, B.R. (1998). Indian Intervention In Sri Lanka: ANATOMY OF A FAILURE. World Affairs: The Journal of International Issues, [online] 2(3), pp.132–145. Available at: https://www.jstor.org/stable/45064546.

FACTBOX-India's role in Sri Lanka's civil war. (2008). Reuters. [online] 17 Oct. Available at: https://www.reuters.com/article/idUKCOL223047.

Korbel Journal, J., Abitol, A. and Abitbol, A. (1962). Sino-Indian War: A systems Level Approach. Josef Korbel Journal of Advanced International Studies, [online] 1, pp.74–88. Available at: https://digitalcommons.du.edu/cgi/viewcontent.cgi?article=1000&context=advancedintlstudies.

Levi, W. (1963). The Sino-Indian Border War. Current History, [online] 45(265), pp.136–143. Available at: https://www.jstor.org/stable/45310978.

BURKE, S.M. (1963). The Sino-Indian Conflict. Journal of International Affairs, [online] 17(2), pp.200–211. Available at: https://www.jstor.org/stable/24381373.

India Today (2016). India-China War of 1962: How it started and what happened later. [online] India Today. Available at: https://www.indiatoday.in/education-today/gk-current-affairs/story/india-china-war-of-1962-839077-2016-11-21.

The Times of India (n.d.). 'Non-alignment' was coined by Nehru in 1954 | India News - Times of India. [online] The Times of India. Available at: https://timesofindia.indiatimes.com/india/non-alignment-was-coined-by-nehru-in-1954/articleshow/2000656.cms.

Nanda, B.R. (1998). Nehru and Non-Alignment. Jawaharlal Nehru, pp.222–249. doi:https://doi.org/10.1093/acprof:oso/9780195645866.003.0012.

Ghoble, T.R. (1997). THE OPIUM WAR & CHINA- INDIA MISUNDERSTANDING. Proceedings of the Indian History Congress, [online] 58, pp.808–818. Available at: https://www.jstor.org/stable/44144026.

Thampi, M. (n.d.).Indian Soldiers, Policemen and Watchmen in China in the Nineteenth and Early Twentieth Centuries. [online] Available at: https://indiachinainstitute.org/wp-content/uploads/2009/07/madhavi-thampi.pdf.

Palsetia, J.S. (2008). The Parsis of India and the opium trade in China. Contemporary Drug Problems, 35(4), pp.647–678. doi:https://doi.org/10.1177/009145090803500408.

Tudor, M. (2023). Why India's Democracy Is Dying. [online] Journal of Democracy. Available at: https://www.journalofdemocracy.org/articles/why-indias-democracy-is-dying/.

Time. (2023). India's Worsening Democracy Makes It an Unreliable Ally. [online] Available at: https://time.com/6288505/indias-worsening-democracy-makes-it-an-unreliable-ally/.

Tellis, A.J. (2022). 'What Is in Our Interest': India and the Ukraine War. [online] Carnegie Endowment for International Peace. Available at: https://carnegieendowment.org/2022/04/25/ what-is-in-our-interest-india-and-ukraine-war- pub-86961#:~:text=India%27s%20response%20to%20the %20Russian,studied%20public%20neutrality%20toward %20Russia.

Frayer, L. (2023). A year into the Ukraine war, the world's biggest democracy still won't condemn Russia. [online] NPR. Available at: https://www.npr.org/2023/02/20/1156478956/russia-india- relations-oil-modi-putin.

JC, A. (2023). India turns a deaf ear to West by paying Russia more for its own gains. The Economic Times. [online] 5 Oct. Available at: https://economictimes.indiatimes.com/news/economy/foreign- trade/india-turns-a-deaf-ear-to-west-for-paying-russia-more-for- its-own-gains/articleshow/104179510.cms?from=mdr.

The Indian Express. (2023). Indian oil firms want their $600 million stuck in Russia to be used for payments to Moscow. [online] Available at: https://indianexpress.com/article/business/ companies/indian-oil-firms-explore-using-stranded-600-million- to-buy-russian-oil-8939952/.

POLITICO. (2023). India has Russia over an oil barrel. [online] Available at: https://www.politico.eu/article/india-has-russia- kremlin-over-crude-oil-barrel/.

AFP (2023). Indian State-owned firm sold artillery barrels to Myanmar: activists. The Hindu. [online] 1 Mar. Available at: https://www.thehindu.com/news/international/indian- state-owned-firm-sold-artillery-barrels-to-myanmar-activists/ article66568081.ece.

Radio Free Asia. (n.d.). India sells arms to junta while claiming concern over crisis in Myanmar. [online] Available

at: https://www.rfa.org/english/news/myanmar/
arms-07032023152856.html#:~:text=Indian%20arms
%20manufacturer%20Bharat%20Electronics.

Radio Free Asia. (n.d.). India is keeping close ties with Myanmar,
even transferring weapons, NGOs say. [online] Available
at: https://www.rfa.org/english/news/myanmar/india-
burma-02222023180530.html.

Kugelman, M. (2023). India Steps Up Diplomacy With
Myanmar. [online] Foreign Policy. Available at: https://
foreignpolicy.com/2023/07/19/india-myanmar-diplomacy-
border-engagement-manipur/.

dw.com. (n.d.). What is India's relationship to Myanmar's military
junta? – DW – 08/02/2022. [online] Available at: https://
www.dw.com/en/india-walks-diplomatic-tightrope-on-myanmars-
military-junta/a-62685316.

India exported most arms to Myanmar during 2017-21. (2022).
The Times of India. [online] 25 Apr. Available at: https://
timesofindia.indiatimes.com/india/india-exported-most-arms-to-
myanmar-during-2017-21/articleshow/91069856.cms.

WHAT IS QUAD? (n.d.). Business Standard India. [online] Available
at: https://www.business-standard.com/about/what-is-quad.

Smith, S. (2021). The Quad in the Indo-Pacific: What to Know.
[online] Council on Foreign Relations. Available at: https://
www.cfr.org/in-brief/quad-indo-pacific-what-know.

Brookings. (n.d.). It's time to resuscitate the Asia-Pacific Quad.
[online] Available at: https://www.brookings.edu/articles/its-time-
to-resuscitate-the-asia-pacific-quad/.

The Economist. (n.d.). India's foreign minister on ties with
America, China and Russia. [online] Available at: https://
www.economist.com/asia/2023/06/15/indias-foreign-minister-
on-ties-with-america-china-and-russia.

Chapter 13:

Transparency International (2022). Corruption Perceptions Index. [online] Transparency International. Available at: https://www.transparency.org/en/cpi/2022.

Transparency International (2021). 2021 Corruptions Perceptions Index . [online] Transparency International. Available at: https://www.transparency.org/en/cpi/2021.

Chutel, L. (2022). South Africa's Corruption Inquiry Leaves Few of the Nation's Powerful Unscathed. The New York Times. [online] 23 Jun. Available at: https://www.nytimes.com/2022/06/23/world/africa/south-africa-corruption-jacob-zuma-cyril-ramaphosa.html.

www.wits.ac.za. (n.d.). 2023-03 - The soul of South Africa: corrupt to the core? - Wits University. [online] Available at: https://www.wits.ac.za/news/latest-news/opinion/2023/2023-03/the-soul-of-south-africa-corrupt-to-the-core.html.

Cloete Murray: South African corruption investigator shot dead. (2023). BBC News. [online] 19 Mar. Available at: https://www.bbc.com/news/world-africa-65007942.

India more corrupt than China, better than Pak: Transparency. (2018). The Economic Times. [online] 22 Feb. Available at: https://economictimes.indiatimes.com/news/economy/indicators/india-more-corrupt-than-china-better-than-pak-transparency/articleshow/63029834.cms.

East Asia Forum. (2023). Countering corruption in India and China. [online] Available at: https://www.eastasiaforum.org/2023/08/26/countering-corruption-in-india-and-china/.

Huang, Y. (2015). The Truth About Chinese Corruption. [online] Carnegie Endowment for International Peace. Available at: https://carnegieendowment.org/2015/05/29/truth-about-chinese-corruption-pub-60265.

Wedeman, A. (2012). *Growth and Corruption in China.* [online] China Research Center. Available at: https://www.chinacenter.net/2012/china-currents/11-2/growth-and-corruption-in-china/.

Wei, Y.D. & S.-J. (2023). *Measuring Corruption in China | by Yongheng Deng & Shang-Jin Wei.* [online] Project Syndicate. Available at: https://www.project-syndicate.org/commentary/study-examines-off-the-book-incomes-of-chinese-officials-by-yongheng-deng-and-shang-jin-wei-2023-09?barrier=accesspaylog.

Deloitte India. (n.d.). *Bribery and Corruption in India | Risk faced by IT companies India.* [online] Available at: https://www2.deloitte.com/in/en/pages/finance/articles/are-it-companies-disbarred-from-the-risks-arising-from-bribery-and-corruption.html.

Sahoo, N. (2022). *India's fight against corruption: A long battle.* [online] ORF. Available at: https://www.orfonline.org/expert-speak/indias-fight-against-corruption/.

Agrawal, A.Kr. (2007). *CORRUPTION IN HISTORICAL PERSPECTIVE : A CASE OF INDIA. The Indian Journal of Political Science,* [online] 68(2), pp.325–336. Available at: https://www.jstor.org/stable/41856330.

NDTV.com. (n.d.). *Opinion: This Is The Seed Of All Corruption In India.* [online] Available at: https://www.ndtv.com/opinion/this-is-the-seed-of-all-corruption-in-india-3420528.

Anon, (2017). *Russia's Weaponization of Corruption (and Western Complicity) – CSCE.* [online] Available at: https://www.csce.gov/articles/russia-s-weaponization-corruption-and-western-complicity/.

Schulze, G.G., Sjahrir, B.S. and Zakharov, N. (2016). *Corruption in Russia. The Journal of Law and Economics,* 59(1), pp.135–171.

doi:https://doi.org/10.1086/684844.

Holmes, L. (2008). Corruption and Organised Crime in Putin's Russia. Europe-Asia Studies, [online] 60(6), pp.1011–1031. Available at: https://www.jstor.org/stable/20451570.

Meijer, N.L., Peter (n.d.). Russian Corruption Is an Urgent Security Threat. [online] Foreign Policy. Available at: https://foreignpolicy.com/2022/07/05/russia-corruption-security-threat/.

Felter, C. and Labrador, R.C. (2018). Brazil's Corruption Fallout. [online] Council on Foreign Relations. Available at: https://www.cfr.org/backgrounder/brazils-corruption-fallout.

Power, T.J. and Taylor, M.M. (2011). Corruption and Democracy in Brazil: The Struggle for Accountability. [online] JSTOR. University of Notre Dame Press. Available at: https://www.jstor.org/stable/j.ctv19m61t1.

Winter, B. (2017). Brazil's Never-Ending Corruption Crisis: Why Radical Transparency Is the Only Fix. Foreign Affairs, [online] 96(3), pp.87–94. Available at: https://www.jstor.org/stable/44823734.

Watts, J. (2017). Operation Car Wash: The biggest corruption scandal ever? [online] the Guardian. Available at: https://wwArif, I., Khan, L. and Waqar, S., 2020. Does corruption sand or grease the wheels? A case of BRICS countries. Global Business Review, p.0972150920927370.w.theguardian.com/world/2017/jun/01/brazil-operation-car-wash-is-this-the-biggest-corruption-scandal-in-history.

Bitterhout, S. and Simo-Kengne, B.D., 2020. The effect of corruption on economic growth in the BRICS Countries: A panel data analysis (pp. 66-78). Economic and Well-being Research Group.

Van NGUYEN, D. and Duong, M.T.H., 2021. Shadow economy, corruption and economic growth: an analysis of BRICS countries.

The Journal of Asian Finance, Economics and Business, 8(4), pp.665-672.

Sahu, S.K. and Gahlot, R., 2014. Perception about corruption in public servicies: a case of BRICS countries. J Soc Sci Policy Implic, 2, pp.109-24.

Chapter 14:

Coquidé, C., Lages, J. and Shepelyansky, D.L., 2023. Prospects of BRICS currency dominance in international trade. arXiv preprint arXiv:2305.00585.

Zharikov, Mikhail Vyacheslavovich. "Digital Money Options for the BRICS." International Journal of Financial Studies 11, no. 1 (2023): 42.

Molodyko, K., 2020. FRoM RESERVE CuRREnCIES To RESERVES oF CRITICAL GooDS: DESIGnInG A nEw BRICS InTERnATIonAL CuRREnCY. BRICS Law Journal, 7(4), pp.67-84.

O'Kane, C. (2023). What is BRICS? Group of world leaders that considered making a new currency meet to discuss economy - CBS News. [online] www.cbsnews.com. Available at: https:// www.cbsnews.com/news/what-is-brics-group-of-world-leaders- that-considered-making-a-new-currency-meet-to-discuss- economy/.

Fortune. (n.d.). BRICS just invited 6 nations including Saudi Arabia and Iran to join—here's why it increases the prospect of dollar replacement. [online] Available at: https:// fortune.com/2023/08/24/brics-new-6-nations-threat-dollar-de- dollarization/.

Karthikeyan, S. (2023). brics common currency push & expansion plans: where does india stand? The Hindu. [online] 21 Aug. Available at: https://www.thehindu.com/news/international/ brics-common-currency-push-expansion-plans-where-does-india-

stand/article67147734.ece.

Savage, R. (2023). What is a BRICS currency and is the U.S. dollar in trouble? Reuters. [online] 24 Aug. Available at: https://www.reuters.com/markets/currencies/what-is-brics-currency-could-one-be-adopted-2023-08-23/.

reporters, G. staff (n.d.). BRICS expected to roll out deepened cooperation mechanism on currency, in push to reduce reliance on dollar - Global Times. [online] www.globaltimes.cn. Available at: https://www.globaltimes.cn/page/202308/1296313.shtml.

Liu, Z.Z. and Papa, M. (2022). Can BRICS De-dollarize the Global Financial System? Cambridge University Press. doi:https://doi.org/10.1017/9781009029544.

dw.com. (n.d.). BRICS summit: Leaders eye expansion, common currency – DW – 08/23/2023. [online] Available at: https://www.dw.com/en/brics-summit-leaders-eye-expansion-common-currency/live-66606155.

Khan, S. (2023). Brics summit: Why the US dollar will remain dominant despite bloc's push to de-throne it. [online] The National. Available at: https://www.thenationalnews.com/business/2023/08/23/brics-summit-dollar/.

Bordo, M.D. and Eichengreen, B., 1998. The rise and fall of a barbarous relic: the role of gold in the international monetary system.

Mundell, R., 2012. The case for a world currency. Journal of policy modeling, 34(4), pp.568-578.

Bunjaku, F., Gjorgieva-Trajkovska, O. and Miteva-Kacarski, E., 2017. Cryptocurrencies–advantages and disadvantages. Journal of Economics, 2(1), pp.31-39.

Rice, M., 2019. Cryptocurrency: History, Advantages, Disadvantages, and the Future.

Chapter 15:

Ashby, H., Markey, D., Randolph, K., Sharad, K., Tugendhat, H. and Verjee, A. (2023). What BRICS Expansion Means for the Bloc's Founding Members. [online] United States Institute of Peace. Available at: https://www.usip.org/publications/2023/08/what-brics-expansion-means-blocs-founding-members.

Plessis, C. du, Miridzhanian, A., Acharya, B., Miridzhanian, A. and Acharya, B. (2023). BRICS welcomes new members in push to reshuffle world order. Reuters. [online] 25 Aug. Available at: https://www.reuters.com/world/brics-poised-invite-new-members-join-bloc-sources-2023-08-24/.

The Hindu Bureau. (2023). Explaining the BRICS expansion | Infographics. The Hindu. [online] 5 Sep. Available at: https://www.thehindu.com/news/international/infographics-explaining-the-brics-expansion/article67248395.ece.

euronews. (2023). BRICS invites new members to join economic bloc. [online] Available at: https://www.euronews.com/2023/08/24/brics-invites-argentina-saudi-arabia-egypt-ethiopia-the-emirates-and-iran-to-join-the-bloc.

MIT News | Massachusetts Institute of Technology. (2023). Q&A: The BRICS expansion and the global balance of power. [online] Available at: https://news.mit.edu/2023/taylor-fravel-brics-expansion-0926.

The Independent. (2023). Brics countries agree major expansion as six countries invited to join. [online] Available at: https://www.independent.co.uk/news/world/africa/brics-2023-summit-new-members-saudi-uae-iran-b2398553.html.

www.batimes.com.ar. (n.d.). BRICS membership in doubt as opposition rejects move | Buenos Aires Times. [online] Available at: https://www.batimes.com.ar/news/argentina/argentinas-brics-membership-in-doubt-as-opposition-rejects-move.phtml.

Matamis, J. (2023). UAE entry into BRICS increases its diplomatic and economic options • Stimson Center. [online] Stimson Center. Available at: https://www.stimson.org/2023/uae-entry-into-brics-increases-its-diplomatic-and-economic-options/.

Stuenkel, O. (2023). BRICS Invitation Puts Argentina in a Tough Spot. [online] Foreign Policy. Available at: https://foreignpolicy.com/2023/09/21/brics-membership-argentina-china-russia-brazil-india-elections/.

www.wilsoncenter.org. (n.d.). Argentina and the BRICS: Port in a Storm or Geopolitical Launching Pad? | Wilson Center. [online] Available at: https://www.wilsoncenter.org/blog-post/argentina-and-brics-port-storm-or-geopolitical-launching-pad.

Bloomberg Línea. (2023). Argentina Among Six Nations to Join BRICS in Bloc's First Expansion Since 2010. [online] Bloomberg Línea. Available at: https://www.bloomberglinea.com/english/argentina-among-six-nations-to-join-brics-in-blocs-first-expansion-since-2010/.

Abdelaziz. M. (n.d.). Egyptian Media Reflections on Egypt's Accession to BRICS. [online] The Washington Institute. Available at: https://www.washingtoninstitute.org/policy-analysis/egyptian-media-reflections-egypts-accession-brics#:~:text=On%20August%2024%2C%20South%20African.

Werr, P. (2023). Egypt hopes BRICS entry will lure foreign cash, but analysts counsel patience. Reuters. [online] 25 Aug. Available at: https://www.reuters.com/world/africa/egypt-hopes-brics-entry-will-lure-foreign-cash-analysts-counsel-patience-2023-08-25/.

Gbadamosi, N. (2023). BRICS Expansion Could Help Egypt's Ailing Economy. [online] Foreign Policy. Available at: https://foreignpolicy.com/2023/08/30/brics-expansion-egypt-economy-ethiopia-investment-dollar-china-russia/.

AfricaNews (2023). *Ethiopian Prime Minister hails BRICS membership.* [online] Africanews. Available at: https://www.africanews.com/2023/08/24/ethiopian-prime-minister-hails-brics-membership//.

Osman, I.D. (2023). *BRICS and Ethiopia: A New Frontier in Geopolitical Tug-of-War.* [online] Modern Diplomacy. Available at: https://moderndiplomacy.eu/2023/08/29/brics-and-ethiopia-a-new-frontier-in-geopolitical-tug-of-war/.

BRICS Group Announces New Members, Expanding Its Reach. (2023). The New York Times. [online] 24 Aug. Available at: https://www.nytimes.com/2023/08/24/world/europe/brics-expansion-xi-lula.html.

Naeni, A. and Fathollah-Nejad, A. (2023). *Iran's BRICS membership: 'Hello to the new world'?* [online] Observer Research Foundation. Available at: https://www.orfonline.org/expert-speak/iran-brics-membership/.

Iran hails BRICS membership as 'success for foreign policy'. (2023). The Times of India. [online] 24 Aug. Available at: https://timesofindia.indiatimes.com/world/middle-east/iran-hails-brics-membership-as-success-for-foreign-policy/articleshow/103018051.cms.

Saudi Arabia Seeks Trade Deals, Mulls BRICS Offer to Lift Exports. (2023). Bloomberg.com. [online] 27 Oct. Available at: https://www.bloomberg.com/news/articles/2023-10-27/saudi-arabia-seeks-trade-deals-mulls-brics-offer-to-lift-export.

AP News. (2023). *Iran and Saudi Arabia are among 6 nations set to join China and Russia in the BRICS economic bloc.* [online] Available at: https://apnews.com/article/brics-russia-china-summit-b5900168d165cc78b36d5d5c068b7a50.

Grumet, T. (2015). *New Middle East Cold War: Saudi Arabia and Iran's Rivalry New Middle East Cold War: Saudi Arabia and Iran's*

Rivalry. [online]. Available at: https://digitalcommons.du.edu/cgi/viewcontent.cgi?article=2027&context=etd.

Editors, T. (2022). Iran and Saudi Arabia Battle for Supremacy in the Middle East. [online] World Politics Review. Available at: https://www.worldpoliticsreview.com/israel-iran-saudi-arabia-battle-for-supremacy-in-the-middle-east/.

Marcus, J. (2017). Why Saudi Arabia and Iran are bitter rivals. [online] BBC News. Available at: https://www.bbc.com/news/world-middle-east-42008809.

Siddiqa, A. and Hiro, D. (2019). Review of Cold War in the Islamic World: Saudi Arabia, Iran and the Struggle for Supremacy. Strategic Studies, [online] 39(3), pp.108–110. Available at: https://www.jstor.org/stable/48544314.

News, A.B.C. (n.d.). Saudi Arabia's human rights record may be overlooked over need for cheap oil, groups say. [online] ABC News. Available at: https://abcnews.go.com/International/saudi-arabias-human-rights-record-overlooked-cheap-oil/story?id=83458741.

OHCHR. (n.d.). Iran update on human rights. [online] Available at: https://www.ohchr.org/en/statements/2023/06/iran-update-human-rights.

news.un.org. (2023). Iran: possible crimes against humanity, absence of accountability - top rights expert | UN News. [online] Available at: https://news.un.org/en/story/2023/03/1134782.

Wintour, P. (2023). Iran rights violations amount to crime against humanity, says UN expert. The Guardian. [online] 20 Mar. Available at: https://www.theguardian.com/world/2023/mar/20/iran-rights-violations-crime-against-humanity-un-expert.

OHCHR. (n.d.). International Commission of Human Rights Experts on Ethiopia Finds Reasonable Grounds to Believe that the Federal Government Has Committed Crimes against Humanity in Tigray Region and that Tigrayan Forces Have Committed Serious Human

Rights Abuses, Some Amounting to War Crimes. [online] Available at: https://www.ohchr.org/en/news/2022/09/international-commission-human-rights-experts-ethiopia-finds-reasonable-grounds.

press.un.org. (n.d.). Spotlighting Human Rights Violations in Six Countries, Including Ethiopia, Ukraine, Third Committee Denounces War Crimes, Sexual Violence, Shrinking Civic Space | UN Press. [online] Available at: https://press.un.org/en/2023/gashc4391.doc.htm.

NPR. (2023). Whatever happened in Ethiopia: Did the cease-fire bring an end to civilian suffering? [online] Available at: https://www.npr.org/sections/goatsandsoda/2023/08/29/1196065266/whatever-happened-in-ethiopia-did-the-cease-fire-bring-an-end-to-civilian-suffer.

Ross, A. (2023). Ethiopia just ended one war. Is another one beginning? Reuters. [online] 8 Aug. Available at: https://www.reuters.com/world/africa/ethiopia-just-ended-one-war-is-another-one-beginning-2023-08-08/.

The Economist. (n.d.). Ethiopia risks sliding into another civil war. [online] Available at: https://www.economist.com/middle-east-and-africa/2023/08/15/ethiopia-risks-sliding-into-another-civil-war.

Amr Hamzawy and Amr Hamzawy (2017). Seven Years On: Why Egypt Failed to Become a Democracy. [online] Carnegie Endowment for International Peace. Available at: https://carnegieendowment.org/2017/12/12/seven-years-on-why-egypt-failed-to-become-democracy-pub-75037.

Chapter 16:

Mulyanto, R. (2023). Why Indonesia did not join BRICS. [online] The China Project. Available at: https://

thechinaproject.com/2023/09/15/why-indonesia-did-not-join-brics/.

Llewellyn, A. (n.d.). *Indonesia's absence from bigger BRICS echoes decades of non-aligned policy.* [online] www.aljazeera.com. Available at: https://www.aljazeera.com/economy/2023/8/28/indonesias-absence-from-bigger-brics-echoesdecadesof-non-alignedpolicy.

Umar, A.R.M. (n.d.). *Another BRIC in the wall? Indonesia's BRICS dilemma.* [online] Indonesia at Melbourne. Available at: https://indonesiaatmelbourne.unimelb.edu.au/another-bric-in-the-wall-indonesias-brics-dilemma/.

Chapter 17:

Morocco has not applied to join BRICS - state media. (2023). Reuters. [online] 19 Aug. Available at: https://www.reuters.com/world/africa/morocco-has-not-applied-join-brics-state-media-2023-08-19/.

Harper, P. (2023). *Morocco has never applied to join Brics, and views SA government as 'hostile'.* [online] The Mail & Guardian. Available at: https://mg.co.za/news/2023-08-19-morocco-snubs-brics-and-malicious-sa/.

Black, I. (2005). *All quiet on the Western Sahara front.* The Guardian. [online] 11 Nov. Available at: https://www.theguardian.com/world/2005/nov/11/worlddispatch.ianblack.

The Africa Report.com. (n.d.). *South Africa's unconditional support for Polisario frustrates Rabat.* [online] Available at: https://www.theafricareport.com/300859/south-africas-unconditional-support-for-polisario-frustrates-rabat/.

Kasraoui, S. (2022). *Western Sahara: Morocco Hits Back at South Africa's Hostile Position.* [online] Morocco World News. Available at:

https://www.moroccoworldnews.com/2022/10/351964/western-sahara-morocco-hits-back-at-south-africas-hostile-position.

Chapter 18:

Middle East Monitor. (2023). South Africa: 8 Arab countries request to join BRICS. [online] Available at: https://www.middleeastmonitor.com/20230815-south-africa-8-arab-countries-request-to-join-brics/.

Prange, A. (2023). A new world order? BRICS nations offer alternative to West – DW – 03/27/2023. [online] dw.com. Available at: https://www.dw.com/en/a-new-world-order-brics-nations-offer-alternative-to-west/a-65124269.

www.aa.com.tr. (n.d.). At least a dozen countries interested in joining BRICS: Russian foreign minister. [online] Available at: https://www.aa.com.tr/en/russia-ukraine-war/at-least-a-dozen-countries-interested-in-joining-brics-russian-foreign-minister/2732749.

Mntambo, N. (n.d.). Algeria likely to be among second batch of countries to join BRICS - Godongwana. [online] Eyewitness News. Available at: https://ewn.co.za/2023/08/26/algeria-likely-to-be-among-second-batch-of-countries-to-join-brics-godongwana [Accessed 30 Oct. 2023].

The Cradle. (n.d.). Five Arab states plus Iran among 19 nations ready to join BRICS. [online] Available at: https://new.thecradle.co/articles/five-arab-states-plus-iran-among-19-nations-ready-to-join-brics.

Silk Road Briefing. (2023). Bangladesh Formally Applies To Join BRICS. [online] Available at: https://www.silkroadbriefing.com/news/2023/06/20/bangladesh-formally-applies-to-join-brics/.

Belarus says it has applied to join BRICS club, RIA reports. (2023). Reuters. [online] 25 Jul. Available at: https://www.reuters.com/

world/europe/belarus-says-it-has-applied-join-brics-club-russian-
ria-agency-2023-07-25/.

Bolivia president to attend BRICS summit in bid for new
investment. (2023). Reuters. [online] 31 Jul. Available at: https://
www.reuters.com/world/americas/bolivia-president-attend-brics-
summit-bid-new-investment-2023-07-31/.

Ualikhanova, A. (2023). Kazakhstan Seeks to Join BRICS and
Enhance Trade and Economic Cooperation. [online] The Astana
Times. Available at: https://astanatimes.com/2023/06/
kazakhstan-seeks-to-join-brics-and-enhance-trade-and-economic-
cooperation/.

www.fmprc.gov.cn. (n.d.). Wang Yi Chairs Dialogue of Foreign
Ministers between BRICS and Emerging Markets and Developing
Countries. [online] Available at: https://www.fmprc.gov.cn/
mfa_eng/wjb_663304/wjbz_663308/activities_663312/202205/
t20220520_10690435.html.

Reuters (2023). Algeria applies to join BRICS, would contribute
$1.5 billion to group bank. Reuters. [online] 21 Jul. Available at:
https://www.reuters.com/world/algeria-applies-join-brics-would-
contribute-15-bln-group-bank-2023-07-21/.

Ntungwabona, A. (2023). Algeria Notably Absent from List of New
BRICS Members. [online] Morocco World News. Available at: https://
www.moroccoworldnews.com/2023/08/357243/algeria-notably-
absent-from-list-of-new-brics-members.

Newsroom (2023). Bahrain-BRICS: Perhaps a new history in the
World economy will be launched. [online] Modern Diplomacy.
Available at: https://moderndiplomacy.eu/2023/08/18/bahrain-
brics-perhaps-a-new-history-in-the-world-economy-will-be-
launched/.

New Development Bank. (n.d.). NDB admits Bangladesh as new
member. [online] Available at: https://www.ndb.int/news/
ndb-admits-bangladesh-as-new-member-development-bank-

established-by-brics-begins-membership-expansion/.

Islam Hasib, N. (2023). BRICS expansion: Why Bangladesh could not make it this time. [online] Dhaka Tribune. Available at: https://www.dhakatribune.com/bangladesh/323425/brics-expansion-why-bangladesh-could-not-make-it.

nationthailand. (2023). Joining BRICs would lead to opportunities for Thailand. [online] Available at: https://www.nationthailand.com/thailand/economy/40030500.

Reuters (2023). What is BRICS, which countries want to join and why? Reuters. [online] 21 Aug. Available at: https://www.reuters.com/world/what-is-brics-who-are-its-members-2023-08-21/.

Honduras requests entry to BRICS-led development bank on China trip. (2023). Reuters. [online] 10 Jun. Available at: https://www.reuters.com/world/honduras-requests-entry-brics-led-development-bank-china-trip-2023-06-10/.

Wang J. (n.d.). Honduran president requests entry into New Development Bank of BRICS - Global Times. [online] www.globaltimes.cn. Available at: https://www.globaltimes.cn/page/202306/1292328.shtml.

Dutton J. (2023). BRICS summit: which Middle East states could join powerful bloc? - Al-Monitor: Independent, trusted coverage of the Middle East. [online] www.al-monitor.com. Available at: https://www.al-monitor.com/originals/2023/08/brics-summit-which-middle-east-states-could-join-powerful-bloc.

Alqarout, A. (n.d.). Is BRICS really the lifeline Palestine needs? [online] www.aljazeera.com. Available at: https://www.aljazeera.com/opinions/2023/8/28/palestines-betting-on-brics-but-is-brics-betting-on-palestine.

Middle East Monitor. (2023). BRICS summit issues special resolution in favour of Palestine. [online] Available at: https://

www.middleeastmonitor.com/20230721-brics-summit-issues-special-resolution-in-favour-of-palestine/.

www.aa.com.tr. (n.d.). *China welcomes Venezuela's intention to join BRICS.* [online] Available at: https://www.aa.com.tr/en/asia-pacific/china-welcomes-venezuela-s-intention-to-join-brics/2991736.

Venezuela's Maduro Wants China's Support to Join the BRICS. (2023). Bloomberg.com. [online] 10 Sep. Available at: https://www.bloomberg.com/news/articles/2023-09-10/venezuela-s-maduro-wants-china-s-support-to-join-the-brics.

VOV.VN. (2023). *Vietnam follows progress of discussions on expanding BRICS membership.* [online] Available at: https://english.vov.vn/en/politics/vietnam-follows-progress-of-discussions-on-expanding-brics-membership-post1040009.vov.

Nikkei Asia. (n.d.). *BRICS invites 6 countries including Saudi Arabia, Iran into group.* [online] Available at: https://asia.nikkei.com/Politics/International-relations/BRICS-invites-6-countries-including-Saudi-Arabia-Iran-into-group.

Sullivan, B. (2022). *Why Belarus is so involved in Russia's invasion of Ukraine.* NPR. [online] 11 Mar. Available at: https://www.npr.org/2022/03/11/1085548867/belarus-ukraine-russia-invasion-lukashenko-putin.

Trenin, D. (2005). *Moscow's relations with Belarus: An awkward ally.* [online] JSTOR. Available at: https://www.jstor.org/stable/pdf/resrep06940.8.pdf.

Hopkins, V. (2023). *Belarus Is Fast Becoming a 'Vassal State' of Russia.* The New York Times. [online] 22 Jun. Available at: https://www.nytimes.com/2023/06/22/world/europe/belarus-russia-lukashenko.html.

Dow Jones Professional. (n.d.). *Explainer: U.S. Sanctions on Cuba.* [online] Available at: https://www.dowjones.com/professional/risk/

glossary/sanctions/us-sanctions-cuba/.

Council on Foreign Relations. (2023). Timeline: U.S.-Cuba Relations. [online] Available at: https://www.cfr.org/timeline/us-cuba-relations.

Robinson, K. (2021). What Is Hamas? [online] Council on Foreign Relations. Available at: https://www.cfr.org/backgrounder/what-hamas.

Schanzer, J., 2008. Hamas vs. Fatah: the struggle for Palestine. St. Martin's Press.

Litvak, M., 1998. The Islamization of the Palestinian-Israeli conflict: the case of Hamas. Middle Eastern Studies, 34(1), pp.148-163.

Astapenia, R. and Balkunets, D., 2016. Belarus-Russia relations after the Ukraine conflict. Analytical Paper, 5, pp.1-23.

NDTV.com. (n.d.). Explained: Israel-Palestine And A History Of Conflict. [online] Available at: https://www.ndtv.com/world-news/israel-palestine-conflict-hamas-gaza-explained-israel-palestine-and-a-history-of-conflict-4458888.

Reuters (2023). Venezuela inflation accelerating, heightening risk of return to hyperinflation, economists say. Reuters. [online] 5 Jan. Available at: https://www.reuters.com/world/americas/venezuela-inflation-accelerating-heightening-risk-return-hyperinflation-2023-01-05/.

Bull, B. and Rosales, A., 2020. The crisis in Venezuela. European Review of Latin American and Caribbean Studies/Revista Europea de Estudios Latinoamericanos y del Caribe, (109), pp.1-20.

Ellis, R.E., 2017. The collapse of Venezuela and its impact on the region. Military Review, 97(4), pp.22-33.

Heath, O., 2009. Economic crisis, party system change, and the dynamics of class voting in Venezuela, 1973–2003. Electoral

Studies, 28(3), pp.467-479.

Tarver, H.M., 2018. The history of Venezuela. Bloomsbury Publishing USA.

Venezuela's bolivar weakens against the U.S. dollar as inflation rages. (2023). Reuters. [online] 3 Aug. Available at: https://www.reuters.com/markets/currencies/venezuelas-bolivar-weakens-against-us-dollar-inflation-rages-2023-08-03/.

Cheatham, A., Labrador, R.C. and Roy, D. (2023). Venezuela: The Rise and Fall of a Petrostate. [online] Council on Foreign Relations. Available at: https://www.cfr.org/backgrounder/venezuela-crisis.

Philipp, J. (2023). How Corruption in Venezuela Causes Poverty. [online] The Borgen Project. Available at: https://borgenproject.org/corruption-in-venezuela/.

Ayuso, A. (n.d.). Violence, corruption and organized crime in Venezuela. [online] Peace in Progress magazine. Available at: https://www.icip.cat/perlapau/en/article/violence-corruption-and-organized-crime-in-venezuela/.

Thioub, I., Diop, M.C. and Boone, C., 1998. Economic liberalization in Senegal: Shifting politics of indigenous business interests. African Studies Review, 41(2), pp.63-90.

English, E.P., 2016. Senegal: A service economy in need of an export boost (No. 2016/150). WIDER Working Paper.

Schmidt, L. (2023). Honduras Makes Few Advances Against Crime During 6-Month State of Exception. [online] InSight Crime. Available at: https://insightcrime.org/news/honduras-makes-few-advances-against-crime-during-6-month-state-of-exception/.

Maja Stamenkovska (2019). 10 Facts About Violence in Honduras | The Borgen Project. [online] The Borgen Project. Available at: https://borgenproject.org/10-facts-about-violence-in-honduras/.

Satubaldina, A. (2023). BRICS Summit: Kazakhstan's Keen Interest in Deepening Partnership. [online] The Astana Times. Available at: https://astanatimes.com/2023/08/brics-summit-kazakhstans-keen-interest-in-deepening-partnership/.

Sánchez, W.A. and Romanov, R. (2023). BRICS Expansion: Gauging Kazakhstan's Potential. [online] Geopolitical Monitor. Available at: https://www.geopoliticalmonitor.com/brics-expansion-gauging-kazakhstans-potential/.

Kelley, C. (n.d.). New report documents human rights abuses in Bolivia. [online] Harvard Law School. Available at: https://hls.harvard.edu/today/new-report-documents-human-rights-abuse-in-bolivia/.

Platt, T. (1988). Cuba and the Politics of Human Rights. Social Justice, [online] 15(2 (32)), pp.38–54. Available at: https://www.jstor.org/stable/29766406.

Garfield, R. and Santana, S., 1997. The impact of the economic crisis and the US embargo on health in Cuba. American Journal of Public Health, 87(1), pp.15-20.

Mesa-Lago, C. and Svejnar, J., THE CUBAN ECONOMIC CRISIS.

Spadoni, P., 2012. Cuban Economic Policies, 1990-2010: Achievements and Shortcomings (pp. 168-90). Nueva York: Oxford University Press.

Chapter 19:

Dixon, H. (2023). Breakingviews - The BRICS are better off disbanding than expanding. Reuters. [online] 31 Jul. Available at: https://www.reuters.com/breakingviews/brics-are-better-off-disbanding-than-expanding-2023-07-31/.

Irrawaddy, T. (2023). Myanmar Junta Eyeing BRICS Membership as Sanctions Bite. [online] The Irrawaddy. Available at: https://www.irrawaddy.com/news/myanmars-crisis-the-world/myanmar-junta-eyeing-brics-membership-as-sanctions-bite.html.

Roelf, W. (2023). BRICS meet with 'friends' seeking closer ties amid push to expand bloc. Reuters. [online] 2 Jun. Available at: https://www.reuters.com/world/brics-meet-with-friends-seeking-closer-ties-amid-push-expand-bloc-2023-06-02/.

Club of Mozambique (n.d.). Angola: Foreign minister warns of challenges to join BRICS. [online] Club of Mozambique. Available at: https://clubofmozambique.com/news/angola-foreign-minister-warns-of-challenges-to-join-brics/.

Devonshire-Ellis, C. (2022). The New Candidate Countries For BRICS Expansion. [online] Silk Road Briefing. Available at: https://www.silkroadbriefing.com/news/2022/11/09/the-new-candidate-countries-for-brics-expansion/.

Herald, T.K. (n.d.). The Korea Herald. [online] www.koreaherald.com. Available at: https://www.koreaherald.com/view.php.

MH NEWS, (2023). Nicaragua Interested In Joining BRICS To Promote Multipolar World, Unity - Top Diplomat - MH NEWS. [online] Available at: https://mhnews.pk/nicaragua-interested-in-joining-brics-to-promote-multipolar-world-unity-top-diplomat/.

OilPrice.com. (n.d.). Emerging Markets Rush To Join BRICS Alliance As High Energy Prices Persist. [online] Available at: https://oilprice.com/Geopolitics/International/Emerging-Markets-Rush-To-Join-BRICS-Alliance-As-High-Energy-Prices-Persist.html.

thediplomat.com. (n.d.). No One Knows What BRICS Expansion Means. [online] Available at: https://thediplomat.com/2023/10/no-one-knows-what-brics-expansion-means/.

Council of Councils. (n.d.). The BRICS Summit 2023: Seeking an Alternate World Order? [online] Available at: https://www.cfr.org/councilofcouncils/global-memos/brics-summit-2023-seeking-alternate-world-order.